HOT
MARKETING,
COOL
PROFITS

200 proven sales and marketing
ideas to grow your business

ROGER BROOKSBANK

The McGraw-Hill Companies, Inc.

Sydney New York San Francisco Auckland
Bangkok Bogotá Caracas Hong Kong
Kuala Lumpur Lisbon London Madrid
Mexico City Milan New Delhi San Juan
Seoul Singapore Taipei Toronto

McGraw·Hill Australia

A Division of The **McGraw·Hill** Companies

National Library of Australia Cataloguing-in-Publication data:

Brooksbank, Roger, 1957–.
Hot marketing, cool profits : 200 proven sales and
marketing ideas to grow your business.

ISBN 0 074 71159 8.

1. Marketing – Handbooks, manuals, etc.
2. Small business – Growth. I. Title.

658.8

Published in Australia by
McGraw-Hill Australia Pty Ltd
Level 2, 82–84 Waterloo Road, Macquarie Park NSW 2113, Australia
Acquisitions Editor: Javier Dopico
Production Editor: Alice Drew
Editor: Sharon Nevile
Proofreader: Tim Learner
Design (interior and cover): Nada Backovic
Illustrator: Diane Booth
Typeset in Goudy and Frutiger by Prototype Pty Ltd
Printed on 70 gsm bulky woodfree by Pantech Ltd, Hong Kong.

CONTENTS

Preface ix

Acknowledgments... x

Introduction xi

Chapter 1   Ideas for growing a customer-driven business   1

1   Make customer satisfaction your top priority............................ 3

2   Make satisfying customers part of everybody's job
     description.. 3

3   Sell the benefits of being customer-driven to your staff 4

4   Develop a customer-driven mission statement......................... 5

5   Use posters to promote customer awareness internally............ 6

6   Lead from the front!... 7

7   Create your own in-company marketing learning resource 8

8   Aim to score some early wins 9

9   Recruit customer champions to help you spread the message . 9

10   Get everyone listening to customers 10

11   Encourage customer visits... 11

12   Cultivate creativity among your staff 12

13   Hold regular brainstorming sessions 12

14   Set up teams of customer owners.. 13

15   Reward customer-first initiatives 14

16   Involve your people in every aspect of sales and marketing
     planning 14

17   Provide one-to-one training for frontline staff......................... 15

Chapter 2   Ideas for conducting savvy market research   17

18   Do some desk research 19

19   Pick the brains of an industry expert....................................... 20

20   Bring your new product concept to life on the Net................. 21

21   Visit an information supermarket in your industry 22

22   Carry out some depth interviews... 23

23   Run a focus group... 25

24   Run an online focus group.. 26

25   Conduct a postal survey.. 27

26   Conduct an online survey... 29

27   Interview by telephone 30

28   Turn your research project into a student research project 31

29   Look into the future with a PEST analysis 33

Chapter 3　Ideas for formulating a winning marketing strategy　35

30　Identify your company's distinctive competencies 37
31　Make the most of your company's marketing assets 37
32　Analyse and segment the market 39
33　Find the right target market 40
34　Focus and concentrate your company's marketing effort 41
35　Become a market rule-maker, not a rule-taker 42
36　Apply the formula S = HVTC + LCTY 43
37　Clearly define your competitive advantage 44
38　Sell only what customers need and want 45
39　Set longer and shorter term marketing objectives 46
40　Always do your sums 47
41　Think until it hurts! 48

Chapter 4　Ideas for providing better company information materials　49

42　Animate your sales brochure 51
43　Support your brochure with an audio tape 52
44　Computerise your product information 53
45　Enclose a company biography with your information pack 54
46　Enclose a supplier evaluation check with your information pack 55
47　Provide staff profiles 55
48　Try the alternative quotation technique 56
49　Consider a very simple web site 57
50　Arm your salespeople with product checklists 59
51　Send out company postcards 60
52　Hand out better business cards 60
53　Improve your letterhead 61

Chapter 5　Ideas for attracting great publicity　63

54　Send out lots of news releases 65
55　Try seminar selling 65
56　Create an award 66
57　Harness local government power 66
58　Wrestle with a crocodile! 67
59　Conduct a phoney feud 68
60　Try the free lunch publicity pact 68
61　Use product placements 69

62 Offer your services to the media as an industry expert 70
63 Write a one-page article 70
64 Produce a book 71
65 Be a good corporate citizen 72
66 Organise a hole-in-one challenge 73
67 Launch a sticker campaign 74
68 Organise a fundraiser 75

Chapter 6   Ideas for advertising more creatively   77
69 Try the information pack prospector 79
70 Activate your print advertising 79
71 Run a word-game poster campaign 80
72 Make every 25th customer a winner! 81
73 Do a deadline deal 82
74 Share your advertising with customers 82
75 Record tele-message ads 83
76 Make the most of directory advertisements 83
77 Try the second-hand prospector method 84
78 Offer a front-end trade-in 85
79 Offer a back-end trade-in 85
80 Make yours a prized product 86
81 Try cinema advertising 87
82 Make the most of your signage 88
83 Blow them away with a blow-out sale 89
84 Try the cartoon-style newspaper ad 90
85 Place advertorials in large companies' newsletters 91
86 Advertise a free information booklet 92
87 Consider the two-part radio ad 93
88 Feature yourselves in a feature page ad 94
89 Advertise on other companies' web sites 95

Chapter 7   Ideas for using direct mail more effectively   97
90 Conduct testing trials 99
91 Run a questionnaire campaign 99
92 Try the three-dimensional exhibition close 100
93 Try doing a post office box-out 101
94 Launch a midnight fax attack! 102
95 Do a boomerang video shot 103
96 Post out a post-it shot 103
97 Use the discount pack method 104

98   Send out customer-get-customer letters 105
99   Try doing the lost letter drop 105
100 Post out some repeater shots.................................... 107
101 Bounce back a special offer to new customers 108
102 Use the market research briefings technique 108
103 Do an old prospects blitz.................................... 109
104 Try the sell through technique 109
105 Use the crumpled postcard flyer 110
106 Email an email shot 111

Chapter 8   Ideas for becoming an expert sales prospector 113
107 Do some piggyback trade show prospecting 115
108 Ask for a referral with every customer you meet 115
109 Arrange a breakfast focus group............................ 116
110 Woo them with a wooing survey.......................... 116
111 Always be on dictaphone duty 117
112 Use the networking memory jogger....................... 117
113 Get into viral marketing................................. 118
114 Build a network of influential contacts 120
115 Become a regular public speaker........................ 120
116 Harness scrapbook power........................... 120
117 Search your local library for sales leads 121
118 Conduct lead-generating competitions among staff 121
119 Use the appointment-getting close 122
120 Set up a voucher partnership.......................... 122
121 Post out a mystery tape 123
122 Do an after hours voice-mail blitz 123
123 Use Alastair's magic cold-calling card method 124
124 Issue introductory discount cards.......................... 125
125 Confirm every sales appointment with a PS letter 126

Chapter 9   Ideas for closing more sales face-to-face 129
126 Adopt a customer-oriented selling approach........................... 131
127 Prepare for every sales visit.......................... 131
128 Make a mental movie of your next sale 132
129 Control your self-talk............................ 133
130 Do the handshake 1–2–3 133
131 Set an agenda... 134
132 Make good use of the customer's name 135
133 Understand the language of silent selling 135

134 Take the time to interview your customer 136
135 Trigger your customer's imagination 137
136 Become an expert listener 138
137 Sell matching benefits 139
138 Make yourself an indispensable component of your offer 139
139 Look out for buying signals 140
140 Ask plenty of trial closing questions 141
141 Master the direct close 141
142 Treat an objection as an opportunity 142
143 Overcome price objections by adding, subtracting, dividing
     and multiplying 143
144 Use the 'try before you buy' close 144
145 Try the ATTACK formula 145
146 Sell add-ons whenever you can 146

**Chapter 10   Ideas for negotiating more profitable sales
                 face-to-face   147**
147 Establish a climate of agreement 149
148 Know your bottom line 149
149 Identify all the non-price variables important to
     your buyer 149
150 Explore the personal interests of the buyer 151
151 In making your opening proposal, aim high 151
152 Trade concessions—don't give them away! 151
153 Never say yes to the buyer's first proposal 152
154 Look out for the 'If I buy this, and this ...' tactic 153
155 Exercise your expertise power 153
156 Conceal your emotions 154
157 Harness print power 154
158 Keep price breakdown information to yourself 155
159 Use the 'continuous-yes' summary close 155
160 Always do some paperwork 156
161 Congratulate the buyer! 157
162 Leave the door open whenever there's an impasse 157

**Chapter 11   Ideas for building stronger customer
                 relationships   159**
163 Say thanks with thank you slips 161
164 Present commemorative plaques 161
165 Launch a sow and grow competition 162

166 Pay unexpected attentions 162
167 Give away functional freebies 163
168 Develop a service vision 164
169 Stay in touch 165
170 Encourage customer complaints 166
171 Create a privileged customer group 167
172 Run a closed door sale 167
173 Invest in a welcoming board 168
174 Be accessible 24/7 169
175 Launch a frequent buyer program 169
176 Follow up everything with a telephone call 170
177 Start a mini-newsletter 171
178 Provide an enewsletter service 172
179 Use telephone stickers 173
180 Provide video reminders of your hospitality events 174
181 Do more than you get paid for 175
182 Create a directory of recommended suppliers 176
183 Distribute people pictures 177
184 Offer a telephone helpline service 178

**Chapter 12   Ideas for controlling your company's overall
             marketing effort**   181

185 Use a performance tracker 183
186 Conduct win and lose reviews 184
187 Monitor customer satisfaction levels 184
188 Make the most of sales force reporting procedures 186
189 Use standard telephone inquiry pads 186
190 Run a marketing intelligence gathering competition 187
191 Measure customer loyalty 188
192 Weed out your unprofitable customers 189
193 Analyse your moments of truth 190
194 Invest in a computerised marketing database 191
195 Use management observation checklists 193
196 Encourage frontline staff to monitor their own performance .. 194
197 Have a 'have your say' day 194
198 Find a way of capturing customer information 195
199 Hire a mystery shopper 197
200 Evaluate every new idea you try 198
     The end piece 199

PREFACE

Deciding on a book title isn't supposed to be easy. The 'selling proposition' must be concisely stated, and in such a way that it appeals directly to target customers. Yet in this case it couldn't have been easier. 'Lots of hot ideas for making cool profits' quipped one of my book reviewers. Hey presto!

In over 20 years of involvement with small businesses, time and again small business owner–managers have told me that the kind of sales and marketing book they really need is a comprehensive 'toolkit' of practical ideas that can be readily applied to their businesses. What's more, a book that is quick and easy to read, full of examples, and one that can be referred to again and again as a source of new ideas and inspiration.

So here it is. A toolkit of practical sales and marketing ideas to help your business grow. I hope you find it useful, and I wish you every success.

Roger Brooksbank

ACKNOWLEDGMENTS

Thanks go to all of the following for making a contribution, in one way or another, towards the writing of this book:

John Clarke
Jeremy Edwards
Brian Marshall
Steve Kane
Nathalie Giraud
Mike Bottomley
Paul McLaughlin
Peter Jones
David Kirby
James McIntosh
Michelle Pinkerton
Michelle Smith
Ning Zhang
Andrew Morgan
Richard Morgan
Zahed Subhan
David Taylor
Alastair Marshall
Vicki Collier
Sophie Cotter
Mark Lytham
Martin Kelly
Sally Board
Margaret Brooksbank
Duncan Steel
Andrea Steel
Neil Lynn
Michele Lynn
Mary FitzPatrick
Merryn Dunsmuir
and especially, Janine Evans

INTRODUCTION

Why you should read this book, and how to get the most out of it

If you are currently involved in running a small business, either as an owner–manager or as a sales and marketing executive, or if you are planning to start your own small business, then this book has been written especially for you.

On the basis of my extensive consultancy work with small companies from around the world, together with my own experiences as a businessperson, I am convinced there are 12 key areas of sales and marketing activity which are crucial to the success of any small business. In fact, I would say that an ability to excel in each of these areas is what sets apart the winners from the rest. Let's take a look at what these areas are, and what's involved.

1. AN ABILITY TO GROW A CUSTOMER-DRIVEN BUSINESS

A customer-driven business is one in which there is a company-wide commitment to satisfying customers.

Owner–managers of successful small businesses continually motivate, inspire and encourage all their employees to make customer satisfaction a top priority in everything they do.

2. AN ABILITY TO CONDUCT SAVVY MARKET RESEARCH

Market research is the process of obtaining specific information from the marketplace for the purpose of making better quality decisions about what to sell, to whom and in what way.

Owner–managers of successful small businesses know that, realistically, no amount of 'gut feel' and 'industry experience' is a substitute for conducting proper research. Customer needs cannot be met unless they are fully understood.

3. AN ABILITY TO FORMULATE A WINNING MARKETING STRATEGY

Formulating a winning marketing strategy involves the careful 'positioning' of a product or service in the marketplace so that it has a unique appeal to a certain group of target customers and is difficult for competitors to copy.

Owner–managers of successful small businesses do not pursue a strategy of trying to be 'all things to all people'. On the contrary, they define a target group of customers to whom they can make an irresistible offer.

4. AN ABILITY TO PROVIDE BETTER INFORMATION MATERIALS

The term 'information materials' refers to all standard letters, brochures, leaflets, booklets, information packs, web sites and other methods of disseminating company information as an aid to the sales process.

Owner–managers of successful small businesses realise that these kinds of materials present a real opportunity to stand out from the competition and be noticed.

5. AN ABILITY TO ATTRACT GREAT PUBLICITY

Publicity involves the securing of free 'air space' in any relevant media such as newspapers, magazines, trade journals, public speaking forums and radio or television, for the specific purpose of building company/product name awareness in the marketplace.

Owner–managers of successful small businesses understand that, for them, the most cost-effective and credible way to build and maintain a high level of name awareness is not by advertising or any other form of paid-for promotion; but through the use of publicity.

6. AN ABILITY TO ADVERTISE MORE CREATIVELY

Advertising is the use of paid-for space in the mass media, such as in a magazine, a trade journal, a newspaper, or on radio or television, for the purpose of communicating with a company's target customers and persuading them to take some form of action.

Owner–managers of successful small businesses take the view that, when it comes to advertising, trying to out-think their competitors by seeking to be creative and different is much more preferable than trying to out-spend them!

7. AN ABILITY TO USE DIRECT MAIL MORE EFFECTIVELY

Direct mail involves the mailing of some form of promotional material direct to selected existing customers and/or prospective new customers, for the purpose of securing repeat business or generating new sales leads.

Owner–managers of successful small businesses understand the importance of personalised, one-to-one communication. Consequently, they direct a constant flow of highly targeted offers to selected groups of both existing and prospective customers.

8. AN ABILITY TO BECOME AN EXPERT SALES PROSPECTOR

The term 'sales prospecting' refers to a systematic approach to identifying potential customers, using a variety of methods that rely purely on the individual efforts of the businessperson.

Owner–managers of successful small businesses make the most of a wide range of sales prospecting methods to generate a constant stream of high quality, low cost sales leads.

9. AN ABILITY TO CLOSE MORE SALES FACE-TO-FACE

Effective face-to-face selling involves the use of a wide range of persuasion and interpersonal communication skills for the purpose of making sales.

Owner–managers of successful small businesses perform an important role as salespeople. They know how to sell, and they know how to do it professionally.

10. AN ABILITY TO NEGOTIATE MORE PROFITABLE SALES FACE-TO-FACE

Sales negotiation is an important aspect of face-to-face selling that takes place whenever the buyer becomes committed in principle to making a purchase, but then starts to argue over terms and conditions. It takes the form of a 'trading and exchange' process for the specific purpose of identifying a mutually acceptable price–package combination.

Owner–managers of successful small businesses know how important it is to be fully prepared for the negotiation phase of the sale—not least because most professional buyers are highly trained negotiators armed with a whole range of tactics for squeezing the lowest possible price out of ill-prepared salespeople.

11. AN ABILITY TO BUILD STRONG CUSTOMER RELATIONSHIPS

The term 'customer relationships' refers to the extent to which there is a feeling of relatedness and rapport between a company and its customers.

Owner–managers of successful small businesses attach a high priority to making sure their customers keep coming back. They know that selling to an existing customer is far more cost-effective than chasing a potential new one. So a lot of time and effort is devoted to keeping in touch with customers, building relationships, and making sure they are always completely satisfied.

12. AN ABILITY TO CONTROL THE COMPANY'S OVERALL MARKETING EFFORT

Marketing control is the process of measuring how well a company and its staff are performing as time goes by, so that any corrective actions can be taken as and when necessary.

Owner–managers of successful small businesses work on the basis that, in a rapidly changing and increasingly competitive world, their strategies and operations should be constantly reviewed. In particular, they keep a watchful eye on any newly emerging marketing opportunities or threats.

As you will see, I have divided this book into 12 separate chapters, each of which deals exclusively with one of these 12 key areas of successful small business marketing. My aim is to provide you with a list of prescriptive ideas (and how-to-do-its) for improving your performance in each area. This means you won't have to read through numerous pages of text hoping to glean one golden nugget of an idea, because in this book they are lined up one after another, chapter by chapter! In fact, there is a grand total of 200 ideas spread throughout the book, and each one carries its own identification number for easy reference.

Despite the number and variety of ideas presented, however, it is important to appreciate that in no way do they represent a definitive listing of good sales and marketing practices, and nor will they all be applicable (or even new) to your business. The intention is simply that you can use them as a basis for getting started on a comprehensive marketing improvement program. By choosing those ideas you think will work best from each of the 12 chapters, you will quickly and easily be able to create an action plan for improving your company's overall sales and marketing performance.

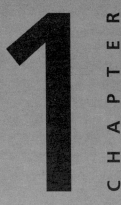

CHAPTER

IDEAS FOR GROWING A
CUSTOMER-DRIVEN BUSINESS

A customer-driven business is one in which there is a company-wide commitment to satisfying customers.

Owner–managers of successful small businesses continually motivate, inspire and encourage all their employees to make customer satisfaction a top priority in everything they do.

Companies are successful in direct proportion to the extent to which they satisfy customers.

① Make customer satisfaction your top priority

If you ask any genuinely successful businessperson what the three most basic ingredients of their marketing success are, I'll wager you'll get an answer that goes something like this:

> *First, it's about satisfying customers—those unreasonable, emotional, and awkward people who only seem to have one saving grace. They give us their money!*
>
> *Second, it's about satisfying customers—those impertinent people who expect us to do things their way, and at their convenience, just because they're paying us!*
>
> *Third, it's about satisfying customers—those disloyal people who, at the drop of a hat, would rather spend their money elsewhere if they think they're going to get better value or a product or service that's more closely tailored to meeting their needs!*

Contrary to what many people think, successful marketing is a lot more than developing a new advertising campaign or this month's promotion. In fact, it runs a lot deeper than just being an exercise in sophisticated persuasion. It is an entire business philosophy, based on the belief that a company's success will be in direct proportion to the extent to which it satisfies its customers. That's why the minute you decide to make customer satisfaction your top priority, you'll be laying the foundations for your company's inevitable success in the marketplace.

② Make satisfying customers part of everybody's job description

The old approach to marketing is epitomised by those owner–managers who think one day that, because sales are slow, perhaps the time has come to 'do' some marketing. So they decide that what their company needs is to take on a marketing executive. Of course, what they have in mind is someone who can polish up the company image a bit, redesign the logo, revamp the advertising campaign, re-do the brochures and generally turn up the volume on the company's promotional effort. Well, that's certainly an important part of marketing, but it's nowhere near the whole story.

Owner–managers who believe success depends on satisfying their customers know they've got to do a lot more than that. In fact, they see marketing as being far too important to leave to just one person, or even one department for that matter. That's why, in a truly marketing-driven company, the task of satisfying customers should be seen as part of everybody's job description. Yes, I mean everybody—from the receptionist to the managing director—because when you think about it, ultimately, everything everyone does in a company affects that company's ability to satisfy its customers. Even those staff who don't serve customers directly are serving someone else in the company who does. So, the first challenge of marketing is to get everyone committed to the principle of customer satisfaction and to ensure all your staff are working together to make it happen.

3 Sell the benefits of being customer-driven to your staff

You will only be successful in building a customer-driven company if everyone wants it to happen. That's why everyone who works for your company must be made aware of the benefits, such as additional repeat business, fewer complaints, less crisis management ('fire fighting'), more new customers by recommendation and, ultimately, greater job security for all.

Use as many promotional approaches as possible to communicate these benefits. For example, you could send everyone a personally signed letter, or launch an internal poster campaign. Most importantly, however, always remember there's no substitute for the good old-fashioned personal approach! Take every opportunity you can to talk to people both individually and as a group, and 'sell' them the benefits of building a more customer-driven business. Above all, appeal to people's hearts and not just their heads. Turn it into a personal issue and try to capture people's imaginations and get them excited. After all, arguably the biggest benefit of all is that in a truly customer-oriented business, people feel a greater sense of involvement in the day-to-day running of the business. Here's an example of how one owner–manager went about doing this:

> In four short years, Computec Ltd had gone from being a new start-up company to becoming a leading supplier of specialised computer systems to the biotechnology industry. The company had six full-time staff, owned its own premises and had a healthy bank balance. However, Tim, the owner–manager of the company, was worried. The market was becoming increasingly competitive and it was getting more difficult to gain repeat

business as well as new clients. He realised that if the business was to survive, let alone prosper, it would have to become more customer-driven and work much more closely with its customers. It seemed everyone at the company was a computer whizz, very technically-oriented but perhaps not as customer-oriented as they could have been. Hence, the 'customerising' process began with a breakfast meeting for all company staff at a local hotel. Tim hired a private room and gave all his staff the full VIP treatment; a silver service breakfast that everyone would remember. He followed this with a 30-minute talk, beginning with a big 'thank you' to everyone for having driven the company's success to date, and an outline of his concerns for the future. This led him smoothly into the main agenda for the meeting—the need for the company to become more customer-oriented and what, in his view, would be the benefits to everyone of building a truly customer-driven future for the company. Tim concluded his talk by encouraging his staff to spend the next hour discussing their attitudes, ideas, training needs and, most importantly, the ways in which they could become more 'customer-conscious' in carrying out their day-to-day activities.

4 Develop a customer-driven mission statement

A mission statement is a clear, long-term vision of what your company stands for, its values and beliefs, and what it is striving to achieve. As such, it can be a powerful tool for driving your company's new customer-oriented business approach, getting all your staff going in the same direction and giving them a common sense of purpose.

Here's an example of a mission statement used by a small firm of marketing consultants:

> To have fun with our clients.
> To make money for our clients.
> To make a difference in our client's business.

The best mission statements are those which are developed *by* employees and not *for* them, because this imparts feelings of ownership and commitment. So get your staff together and develop a well worded mission statement for your company. Here's a good way to get started. In 50 words or less, write down your answers to the following questions:

- *Why are we in business?*
- *Why this product or service?*
- *Who are our customers and what are their needs that we have to meet?*
- *What are the key values and principles by which we conduct our business?*

Remember that a mission statement is basically a promotional tool, so keep it short and sharp and make sure it highlights your new customer orientation. When you've finished crafting your new mission statement, promote it internally by framing it and displaying it on your office and workshop walls. A good tip is to get everyone to sign and date each copy that you display. As you can imagine, this is a great way to cement people's allegiance to your new mission statement!

5 Use posters to promote customer awareness internally

One of the best ways to communicate the importance of being customer-driven to your staff, is to launch an internal poster campaign. Check out the following example:

A friend who works for a large ball-bearing company recently told me the story of how her company's chief executive officer (CEO) had once addressed the entire workforce at their annual sales conferece by getting up on stage and asking everyone, 'Who's your boss?' After a few moments someone shouted out, 'You are', so the CEO promptly wrote his own name down on the overhead projector. Slowly but surely the audience warmed to their task, and the names of supervisors, depot managers, secretaries and other key personnel were called out by various members of the audience, and as they did the CEO diligently wrote them all down in a long list. Eventually, when just about everyone's name had been called out, the CEO stopped writing and with a bright red pen and a dramatic gesture crossed it all out. All of a sudden the auditorium became hushed with silence. 'I'm sorry folks, but you're all wrong,' the CEO exclaimed with a broad smile across his face. 'I'm afraid none of these people are your real boss', at which point he put another slide onto the projector which listed the names of the company's top 500 customers. 'Now,' he said, in a more serious tone, 'from now on, no matter who you are or what you do in this company, I want us all to remember that there's only one real boss around here—and that's our customers! Why? Because it's the customer who pays our wages, it's the customer who pays the bills, and it's the customer who decides if we're going to stay in business next year!'

The really interesting part of this story, however, is what happened next. Apparently for the next few months the CEO followed up his speech with an in-company poster campaign to promote customer awareness to all his staff. Posters were circulated throughout the company based on the theme, 'Who's the boss?' They all featured three lines of writing. The first line was always the same question: 'Who's the boss?', and the second line was always the same answer: 'The customer', but the third line was always a different reason as to why the customer should be seen as the boss (for example: 'Because they pay our wages!' or 'Because we depend on their business' and so on).

Why not use a similar approach in your company? An alternative to producing your own posters is to purchase them 'off the shelf'. They are commercially available and come in all sorts of styles. Whereas some make the point in a very humorous way (for example, by means of a cartoon), others are more serious in nature. Obviously, be sure to choose those you think are most appropriate for your people and those which relate best to your marketplace.

6 Lead from the front!

Remember the old saying 'actions speak louder than words'? Well, when it comes to providing the necessary leadership in growing a truly customer-driven company, I am convinced that actions speak much louder than words! Surely there's nothing more demoralising for staff than when the boss doesn't practise what they preach. That's why it's so important for you as the owner–manager of the business to be seen to be totally committed to your new customer-driven philosophy. In fact, you should be positively buzzing with an enthusiasm which is so contagious that everyone around you is infected by it. Let's say, for example, a customer is due to visit your office. If you know everyone is busy, then let your people see you tidying up the reception area yourself, or let them see you moving your car so the customer can park right outside the front door; whatever it takes!

It's only by leading from the front and showing staff that you, too, are prepared to change the way you do things, and the way you carry out your daily tasks, that you'll ever have any hope of getting them to do the same. Make sure, though, that you're not faking it. Once people catch you not really caring about a goal you've set, it's all over. They'll stop caring because you don't. When it comes to building a customer-driven business you have to *own* the vision and you have to *live* the vision.

⑦ Create your own in-company marketing learning resource

Building a customer-driven company relies completely on the attitudes, knowledge and skills of your staff, so a basic ingredient of success is to train and develop your people. First and foremost, you should aim to change the attitudes of your staff by promoting a deep understanding of the meaning and importance of adopting a customer-oriented business approach. Next, you should aim to improve the overall knowledge and skill levels of your staff in all the functional areas of marketing that relate to their areas of job responsibility (for example, sales and service, market research and so on).

The best training programs integrate a range of teaching and learning methods. Ideally, every program should include in-company training sessions facilitated by company staff themselves, as well as specialist trainers hired from outside agencies. In addition staff should be sent on short courses and seminars run by outside training organisations. Unfortunately, though, all this costs money and small business owner–managers often tell me that although they're committed to the principle of staff training, the truth is that even with the best intentions, they simply can't always afford a proper marketing education program for their people. I must admit that this can be a real problem—formal training programs can easily end up costing a small fortune. However, there is something else you can do. Since there are so many self-help books, instructional tapes, CDs and so on available these days covering a wide range of topics, why not start collecting them and create your own in-company library? All you have to do is to designate a corner cupboard somewhere to be your new 'Marketing Learning Centre' and operate a simple sign-in/sign-out system so that any member of staff can borrow whatever materials they need, as and when they need them. Admittedly it's never going to be a substitute for a proper training program, but it's a great way to improve staff skills. In fact, in my experience, companies that have started using this approach have found it is extremely effective because it puts the responsibility for self-improvement back where it should be; and that's in the hands of each staff member. They can learn at their own pace and in their own time and, more to the point, it means they can do it at virtually no extra cost to the business.

8 Aim to score some early wins

If your company is like most, then it's highly likely that there are a number of obvious areas where a little application could easily make a big difference to your ability to satisfy customers. For example, most companies have some aspect of their product or service that customers seem to complain about constantly yet somehow, inexplicably, nobody has ever bothered to sort it out. Another example might be a problem in your accounting process that causes untold frustration for everybody concerned, but for some reason it has been ignored for months.

Do these kinds of problems sound familiar to you? If they do, then these are precisely the areas you should target early in your new 'customer-first' initiative. By aiming to score some 'early wins' in those problem areas which are well known to everyone and which can be corrected relatively easily, you can guarantee your new initiative will get off to a good start.

9 Recruit customer champions to help you spread the message

If your company is spread over a number of different locations then, no matter how much time and energy you devote to growing a more customer-driven business, there simply won't be enough hours in the day to ensure that, across the whole company, people are taking it seriously. In addition, there will always be at least some resistance from certain people; you know, those who see it as some sort of management trick to get them to work harder, or those who just think the whole thing is a waste of time. So if you're not around to put a stop to it, negativity might take hold. That's why it's a good idea to get as much support as you can by recruiting one or more 'customer champions' to work on your behalf, at ground level.

A customer champion is someone who, just like you, is totally committed to the cause and is prepared to champion it and work tirelessly within their own location to make sure people are actually becoming more 'customer-conscious' in the way they do things. In particular, it's their job to deal with any scepticism or negativity, before it starts infecting people.

The best customer champions are those who are both well respected by their colleagues and obsessed with the cause. However, don't make the mistake of thinking you can appoint your customer champions. It is far better to let your customer champions step out from the ranks and volunteer themselves for the task, so that when you tell them what you'd like them to do, they're positively itching to get on with it, and with the kind of evangelical zeal that's guaranteed to win people over.

10 Get everyone listening to customers

I once came across the following little verse, written by an anonymous author. As you'll see, it's the creed of the truly customer-driven company. You may have seen a similar version elsewhere.

Our customers are not dependent on us,
We are dependent on them!
Our customers are not an interruption to our business,
They are the reason for it!
Our customers don't have to listen to us,
We must listen to them, so they'll keep on coming back!

I like it because it highlights the right kind of attitude that we should have towards our customers. In particular, though, note the emphasis on listening. If we are serious about satisfying customers, shouldn't we be listening more closely to what they tell us about their needs and wants, and about how we can satisfy them better? Yet how often do we fail to really listen to our customers, relying instead on making assumptions about what we think they want?

If this sounds all too familiar, then the first step in getting your people to start listening to customers is to get them into the habit of asking the right questions. Whenever any member of staff has any dealings with a customer, encourage them to take the opportunity to find out more. Sit down with your staff and put together a list of basic questions they should be asking. For example, what do customers think of your product? In what ways could it be improved, and why? How do they feel about the quality of service they have received? What did they think of the purchasing process, installation, delivery, training, invoicing arrangements and so on? Bear in mind that, depending on the particular tasks each member of staff performs, some are going to be better placed than others to collect different types of customer information.

The next step is to make sure that whenever anyone is asking these kinds of questions, they make notes on the answers they are being given.

The best approach is to create a simple questionnaire (for staff use only) which not only reminds staff what questions to ask but also encourages them to make a note of the customer's response. Finally, you'll need to devise a system for disseminating this information among your staff on a regular basis so that you can decide what should be done about it.

11 Encourage customer visits

One of my favourite management books is *Thriving on Chaos* by Tom Peters, and one of the most memorable parts of the book for me is a letter that a manager from the Caterpillar Company wrote to him. Here's an extract from it.

> *Dear Tom,*
> *I have just completed perhaps the most educational month of my business career. I am responsible for the parts department of a large Caterpillar dealership. As part of a renewed emphasis on customer service, I spent some time working in the warehouse of one of our largest customers. What an eye-opener! Being on the receiving end of one of our Caterpillar parts shipments rather than the shipping end was informative, to say the least. I learned firsthand why this customer was complaining, because I was the one who had to open the boxes, sort through the parts and process the paperwork.*

Admittedly, the idea of being able to afford the luxury of spending a whole month working for one of your customers is a bit far-fetched! However, ask yourself this: with the exception of sales and service people, how many of your staff (especially those in administration, accounts or production) ever get to see the light of day, let alone a customer, between 9 a.m. and 5.30 p.m.? In fact, chances are they have worked for so long in the same job that they've actually lost sight of the fact that, if it weren't for customers, they would not have a job at all; lost sight of who your customers really are, and what's important to them; lost sight of the fact that the way they do their jobs ends up affecting the way your customers feel about doing business with your company.

Of course, you don't have to send your staff out to work for a customer for a whole month to remind them of these things. A day's visit or perhaps just a couple of hours would do. Better still, how about getting a customer to visit your offices or factory now and again? Not only does it help keep everyone in tune with what's going on in the marketplace, it's a great way to build personal relationships and show your customers that you really do care about them.

12 Cultivate creativity among your staff

In a truly customer-driven company, staff are always seeking better ways of doing things—ways that will enable the company to better satisfy customers and become more cost-effective in its operations. It is therefore imperative that owner–managers encourage people to realise their creative potential. In facilitating this process it is firstly necessary to identify the creativity barriers, or perceived blocks, that currently exist in your company. Next, decide what can be done to overcome these barriers. Some typical creativity 'blocks' and 'blockbusters' are highlighted below:

- *I don't have enough time to be creative.* Make more time to be creative, and give it a higher priority.

- *I have to follow the rules.* Dismantle any unnecessary rules and policies.

- *I dare not make any mistakes.* Encourage experimentation and banish the fear of failure.

- *I'm not a creative person.* Train staff in the skills and techniques of creativity.

- *I shouldn't be silly.* Embrace non-conformity and fresh ideas.

13 Hold regular brainstorming sessions

Owner–managers often report this as one of their most valuable tools in promoting a 'customer culture'. By holding a regular brainstorming session with the specific goal of answering the question: 'How can we satisfy our customers better?' enthusiasm levels are maintained and lots of bright ideas eventuate—not to mention the fact that everyone feels personally involved in the process of building a more customer-driven business. Here's how to conduct an effective group-brainstorming session.

Assemble half a dozen or so people in a quiet room. The group could be made up of staff that work together in a particular area of the business or, alternatively, a mixture of people drawn from all the various functional areas. You might even want to include someone from outside the business, such as a non-executive director or one of your suppliers or distributors, or perhaps one of your customers with whom you are particularly friendly. (It is always useful to get an outsider's perspective.)

Start off by writing the following question, in large lettering, right across the top of a flip chart or whiteboard: 'How can we satisfy our customers better?' However, always phrase the question in the most specific terms possible so that you can really focus people's attention. For example, if you sell more than one product or service, or if you sell to distinctly different types of customers, then relate the question to one or the other of these. Next, appoint a group leader whose job it is to write out everyone's ideas and to make sure that nobody criticises any idea. The whole point of brainstorming is to try and generate as many ideas as possible. Set a time limit of 15 minutes and start the session by getting everyone involved straight away. This can be done by going around the room and getting one idea from each person. Then, after a couple of circuits, switch to a more unstructured approach, encouraging people to build on each other's ideas at random.

Most importantly, when the session is over, thank everyone for their input and make sure that within a day or so you follow through by telling everyone which ideas you're going to take a step further and how you intend to proceed.

14 Set up teams of customer owners

If your company has at least one major customer who is valuable enough to merit special attention, then this idea can work well in helping to build a customer-driven business approach. It involves setting up a small team of staff and making them 100 per cent responsible for looking after all aspects of your company's dealings with a key customer. It is important, however, that your team of 'customer owners' should be made up of staff members drawn from each of the various functional areas of the business (say one from production, one from finance, one from sales, one from administration and so on). It is also important that team members should continue to carry out their usual duties, devoting only a certain proportion of their time to team activities. In this way, staff members from across the company learn about the need to work together to deliver customer satisfaction, as well as the value of each other's contributions in making it happen. What's more, this kind of team approach is a great way of ensuring that all staff experience a very real sense of responsibility and commitment to satisfying customers. Note that if you have two or three key customers then, ideally, a different team should be assigned to each one so that as many staff as possible have at least some direct involvement with a customer.

15 Reward customer-first initiatives

Whenever anyone initiates a successful new idea that is clearly customer-oriented, always make sure it is properly recognised and rewarded. There are usually two basic components to any reward system. On the one hand, there's the dollar value of the reward itself. For example, this could take the form of cash, tickets to a football match or whatever. On the other hand, there's the recognition component. I'm referring to the warm feeling that a person gets when they know their contribution has been recognised and appreciated by the boss.

When you're using a reward system as a means of encouraging staff to become more customer-conscious, I am convinced that the recognition component is by far the more important of the two (it's also the least expensive!). The reason is that, above all else, people love to feel appreciated! That's why I would always recommend that you use *awards* as rewards. Nothing elaborate, maybe a simple token of appreciation of some kind or just a personally written letter of thanks, signed by the boss, would suffice. The main thing is that it symbolises your recognition of their achievement. In giving an award, you can maximise its effectiveness by following three simple guidelines. First, always award them quickly and spontaneously, whenever you feel it's deserved. Second, make sure it is done publicly in full view of the other members of staff, so your recipient gets the full recognition value among their peers. Third, do it personally, by shaking hands and showing how much you value their contribution, no matter how small it might have been.

16 Involve your people in every aspect of sales and marketing planning

Picture this: It's the company boardroom of a traditional medium-sized manufacturing company. There's a hushed audience of senior managers as a team of three young marketing consultants begin their presentation. There's a buzz of anticipation in the air, because for the last couple of months the three consultants have been working closely with the managing director to produce the company's first ever sales and marketing plan. About half an hour later, having unveiled the plan, the team concludes the meeting by handing over a very impressive-looking, leather-bound copy, to rapturous applause.

Now picture this: It's the same company three months later. For everyone who works there, it's business as usual. The consultants' invoice has long since been paid but, surprisingly, there's been no noticeable change to the company's operations. In fact, the only visible evidence of the company's new sales and marketing plan is the document itself, which has pride of place on the top shelf in the managing director's office!

Now ask yourself this: What's gone wrong? Why is the new plan collecting dust on a shelf and not being used? Well the truth is that, even if this company's plan had been the most brilliant plan in the world, it was destined to fail right from the start because, apart from the managing director, no other members of staff were involved in its formulation. In other words, when the people who are responsible for translating a plan into action aren't involved in its design and development, then it's simply not going to happen. It's a phenomenon known in marketing circles as the SPOTS syndrome, which stands for **S**ales and marketing **P**lan **O**n **T**he **S**helf, because that's exactly what happens when a company's staff haven't been involved in its compilation every step of the way and when there's no feeling of personal involvement, responsibility and commitment among the troops. Be warned! It is impossible to successfully build a customer-driven business without involving your people in every aspect of sales and marketing planning.

17 Provide one-to-one training for frontline staff

In building a customer-driven company, it is of critical importance that your frontline sales and service staff are properly trained. Quite apart from the fact that you need them to be highly effective at what they do, they also hold in the palm of their hands your firm's reputation for being customer-friendly. To put it another way, those staff who deal with customers face-to-face effectively represent the 'public face' of your company, which is why it's necessary to pay extra special attention to their training and professional development. In fact, I believe they're so important that you should take personal responsibility for providing them with one-to-one 'on the job' training in front of the customer. So here's a three-step formula for doing just that:

STAGE ONE: *Show the staff member how to do it. The staff member introduces you to the customer as their boss and then you go on to conduct the entire sale/service session while your staff member sits quietly and* observes. Afterwards, ask your staff member to repeat exactly what you did and how you did it.

STAGE TWO: Do it together. The staff member introduces you to the customer as their boss and then proceeds to conduct the first half of the session before handing over to you. Afterwards, ask your staff member what they could have done better.

STAGE THREE: Let the staff member do it. The staff member introduces you as a colleague, and then you sit quietly and observe while they conduct the entire sale/service session on their own. Afterwards, ask your staff member to analyse and critique their performance.

IDEAS FOR CONDUCTING
SAVVY MARKET RESEARCH

Market research is the process of obtaining specific information from the marketplace for the purpose of making better quality decisions about what to sell, to whom and in what way.

Owner–managers of successful small businesses know that, realistically, no amount of 'gut feel' and 'industry experience' is a substitute for conducting proper research. Customer needs cannot be met unless they are fully understood.

If you think there's a gap in the market, market research will tell you if there's a market in the gap.

18 Do some desk research

Why go to the trouble and expense of collecting information from the marketplace yourself, first hand, if someone else has already been there and got it? As the term implies, 'desk research' is the reviewing of existing published information. In practice, this means searching the Internet, studying at the library and/or doing whatever else it takes to track down useful information from the comfort of a desk. As such, it's an excellent starting point for just about any market research program, but don't take my word for it. Read what one small business owner–manager had to say about the value of desk research in a speech he made recently at an entrepreneurship conference. He was introduced as someone who, a few years earlier, had bought an old derelict brewery, restored it, and then—against all the odds—turned it into a profitable business selling a 'boutique' real ale made the traditional way. He opened his speech by saying:

> When I first got the idea, I had a hunch there'd be sufficient demand among other real ale enthusiasts like me, but in reality I knew nothing at all about the market by way of facts and figures. It was only after I spent a few hours at the library that I became seriously interested in taking the project a stage further. I found out that although the overall beer market had been slowly declining for many years, there was a pocket of growth in the specialist beer market. Although this market was quite small, it was actually growing by about 10 per cent per annum ...

As this example indicates, desk research has got to be the cheapest and most convenient way of getting a 'handle' on a market. From your desk you can access the following types of background information, and more:

- Current market size and worth
- Market trends
- Number of competitors
- Market share figures
- Manufacturing methods and technologies
- Distribution channels

Before doing any desk research it is important to make a list of your information requirements so you know what you're looking for. Next, pick up the telephone and ask as many people as you can if they can point you in the direction of any publications—articles, reports, web sites, fact sheets or whatever—which might give you the information you need. There are numerous organisations worth asking, such as trade associations, chambers of commerce, small business agencies, enterprise centres, consumer organisations, government departments, market research companies, academic researchers and the like. Then start sifting through the literature, and be prepared to follow a paper trail if that's what it takes. To do good desk research it's usually necessary to develop a sort of 'detective's nose' for sniffing out the information you want. However, just like a good detective, if you stick to your task, nine times out of ten you'll be amazed at both the quality and quantity of information that's already out there, somewhere, just ready and waiting for you to stumble across it. One last point. Since published information has been compiled by someone else and for their own reasons, you should always double-check on its relevance and accuracy in relation to your own research objectives.

19 Pick the brains of an industry expert

One of the best 'short cuts' to finding out a lot about a market in a very short time is to seek the opinion of an 'industry expert'. An industry expert is someone who is well respected, wise, knowledgeable and experienced in their field, and someone who has worked in or around an industry over many years. As such, they may well be described as a walking encyclopedia of industry knowledge—a person who is well worth talking to for an hour or two! Examples of industry experts to look out for include journalists, authors, editors, business analysts and other media people, solicitors, accountants, consultants and other professional service providers; as well as other key businesspeople such as distributors, suppliers, salespeople and business owners. Also note that of course it is quite possible that one of your potential customers may well be an industry expert too.

Having identified one or more industry experts who may be able to help you, the next step is to telephone them to request a meeting. When making the call, be sure to explain clearly that you are a small business operator seeking their help in learning more about a specific marketplace and say how much you would appreciate their time. If you put this the right way, most people will be only too pleased to help, especially if you're the one visiting them and doing all the travelling. By the way, on the day of the meeting make sure you are well prepared with a long list of questions. Picking the brains of an industry expert is a wonderful opportunity to learn about what's really going on out there, so be sure to make the most of it.

20 Bring your new product concept to life on the Net

A classic 'catch 22' situation facing many budding entrepreneurs goes something like this:

> Suppose you've come up with a radically new product concept that includes a number of technical innovations. You've done a little homework and a few costings that look quite good. However, you're still very uncertain about its commercial feasibility. So at this point you're simply not prepared to invest what would be a considerable amount of time and money in building a prototype until you've got some detailed feedback from a few industry experts—but the problem is, because of the complex nature of your idea, you're unable to explain it sufficiently well without having some kind of prototype to show them in the first place!

Sound familiar? If so, why not harness the extraordinary capabilities of modern computer graphics to produce a 'virtual prototype' instead of a real one? By creating 3-D images that can be rotated and viewed from all angles you can effectively bring your new product ideas to life on a computer screen. Not only is it relatively quick and easy to do but, best of all, it's ideal for research purposes because a virtual prototype can be transported over the Internet to any destination of your choice within an instant.

Assuming you're able to create a virtual prototype of your new product concept, then making use of it as a research tool is a three-step process. The first step is to telephone the two or three industry experts you've identified as being the best ones to talk to, with a view to gaining some initial feedback about your new product concept. Obviously, an industry expert is someone who is highly respected, knowledgeable and experienced in your industry. However, bear in mind that the best ones to contact are only ever those who you also know to be totally trustworthy and with whom you'd be quite happy to share your new product ideas! When making the calls, be sure to introduce yourself as an independent entrepreneur with an exciting new product idea, and make it clear that the reason for your call is to request their help in evaluating its market potential. Go on to explain that you'd like to send through a virtual prototype of your idea, in the form of an email attachment, so they can view it and evaluate it in their own time and at their own convenience before you telephone them back for an opinion.

The next step is to send each of your industry experts a personalised email message together with the attachment. In the message refer back to your telephone conversation, thank them once again for agreeing to help, and confirm that you've attached the virtual prototype as promised. Most importantly though, take the opportunity to briefly describe your idea and to identify the key issues you'd like them to focus on when conducting their evaluation, such as their thoughts about the practicality of your idea, its potential target customers, its main competitors and so on. In particular, make sure the attachment containing your virtual prototype is presented in a form that makes it as easy as possible to access.

A day or so later, the final step is to telephone each of your industry experts so that you can discuss their reactions to your idea while it is still fresh in their minds. Since they have been able to bring your idea to life on their computer screens, they should now be in a position to give you an informed opinion together with some detailed suggestions, which is why it's well worth making the most of this opportunity by taking your time to prepare your questions carefully before making these calls. You never know, a few well-chosen probing questions might be all it takes to get some brilliant marketing insights or suggestions for improvement.

21 Visit an information supermarket in your industry

The following story clearly illustrates why I believe this idea should form a part of any company's market research program:

> Some time ago I received a telephone call from my old friend Mike, who for many years had run a successful sales training company. He was considering branching out into other forms of management training and

wanted my advice. At the time, the management training industry was rapidly expanding amidst much speculation about how the new generation of interactive computer-based training products would 'revolutionise' the market. In short, Mike was concerned that if he didn't capitalise on some of these new opportunities his company would soon get left behind, but he was unsure about which direction to take. Well, I had to admit to being equally confused. Consequently, seeing as I myself had a keen interest in the changing nature of this market, we decided the best way of learning more would be to attend the next industry trade show together.

Sure enough, a couple of months later we finally made it to one of Europe's largest training expos. Within half an hour of wandering around in the hustle and bustle of just one of four massive exhibition halls, Mike quipped that it was rather like visiting an information supermarket, such was the variety and scale of competitive information available. What an appropriate turn of phrase! Every conceivable type of training company, large and small, as well as every conceivable type of training method, old and new, was represented. Added to that, every conceivable kind of potential customer or user of training products and services was also there, all under the same roof and all happy to discuss their training needs with anyone who might be able to help. Not only that, but as part of the show, there were also seminars led by industry experts talking about all aspects of the training market, providing market facts and figures, and giving their opinions about future trends and developments. All in all, I don't think it would have been possible for Mike and I to have learned more about the marketplace within the space of a day!

When visiting a trade show for market research purposes it usually pays to prepare a 'hit list' of your information requirements before you get there. As you can see from the above example, although trade shows are particularly useful for finding out about competitors' offerings, there's a whole host of other information on offer too, providing you're prepared to go fishing for it. Apart from collecting competitors' brochures, price lists and other handout materials, take the opportunity to pick the brains of as many people as you can, including exhibitors, organisers, speakers and other visitors.

22 Carry out some depth interviews

A 'depth interview' is a face-to-face discussion with a customer to find out as much as possible about a specific area of interest. In particular, it's a great research tool when you need to gain a deeper understanding of a customer's thoughts, feelings, attitudes and behaviour, or when you want to find out more about a particularly sensitive topic area. It's especially useful if you want to show the customer something, such as a prototype or some planned advertising material, in order to get some specific feedback.

Although you wouldn't typically need to conduct more than a handful of depth interviews they are, nevertheless, extremely time-consuming. However, the richness of information and insight that can be gained from using this approach usually proves to be well worth the time invested, not to mention the opportunity it gives you to 'network' and develop some valuable industry contacts. Here's an example of this idea in action:

> An entrepreneur was considering importing a new type of health food product, but wanted to gauge the level of market interest before committing himself to purchasing a trial shipment. To do this, he decided the best form of market research would be to conduct some depth interviews with the chief buyers from four of the largest chains of health food stores in his region. First, he telephoned to make an appointment to visit each one at their office. Then, on the day of the interviews, he took along a product sample together with a list of pre-prepared questions designed to:
> - gauge the buyer's initial reaction to the product
> - find out if they thought there would be a demand for it, and if so, who they thought the customers were likely to be
> - determine the buyer's willingness to stock the product, and their thoughts about its advertising, promotion, packaging, pricing and in-store merchandising
> - identify which products it would compete with, in-store
> - understand the nature of the buyers' decision-making processes, as well as any special contractual stipulations.

As you will appreciate, before meeting up with your interviewees, it's essential that you prepare a discussion guide in the form of a detailed checklist of all the key points you want to cover, and in a logical sequence. This will ensure you won't forget anything, and that each interviewee is asked for basically the same information and in a similar fashion. A good tip is to print it up with plenty of white space between each item on your checklist, because this makes it easy to jot down notes during the interview. In a one-to-one interview I find this method of data capture preferable to using a tape recorder, which can easily put people off.

At the interview itself, start off by setting the scene with a brief explanation of your objectives, a mention of the time you expect it will take (usually about an hour), and a big thank you for their time. Create a friendly and relaxed atmosphere throughout the interview, and keep probing for as much detailed information as you can by asking lots of open questions that begin with the words: who, what, when, where, how and why? At the conclusion of the discussion, thank your interviewee once again, and try to leave the door open for any follow-up that may be required.

One last point. A question I'm often asked is: 'How many interviews should I conduct?' Well of course this is largely a question of personal judgement. However, a good tip is to continue doing them until the answers are becoming repetitive and a pattern of responses seems to have been established. At this point it's highly likely that the information you are getting is going to be truly representative of any larger population under investigation.

23 Run a focus group

A focus group is formed of seven or eight participants who have been especially selected to reflect the make-up of a target market. This group is gathered together for the purpose of facilitating a relaxed and free-flowing discussion about their ideas, thoughts and opinions surrounding a specific marketing decision area. As such, focus groups are particularly useful when exploring the market potential for a new product or service concept, or when you are thinking of redesigning or improving your existing product or service. The main advantage of this research method is that the dynamics of the group tends to get participants talking much more freely than they normally would, thereby generating a lot of rich information relatively inexpensively and within a very short space of time. However, it should be noted that the quality of information generated will depend largely on your skills as a facilitator, and your ability to control and guide the discussion in the right direction. Here's an example of one entrepreneur's use of focus group research:

At last it seemed the time had come for Graham to quit his job and start his business. After many years working in his spare time he had finally perfected his invention—a treatment process that turned ordinary garden refuse into high grade compost in double quick time. What's more, his business idea seemed infallible: for a small subscription he would provide an ongoing garden refuse collection and disposal service for householders, process the waste and then sell on the compost to the trade. However for all that, Graham was worried about the true feasibility of his plan and still had many unanswered questions.

Everything hinged on there being a market for his refuse collection service, but would there be one? Who would be his target customers? What benefits would they see in his scheme? How much might they be prepared to pay? How would the collection service actually work? To find out, Graham decided to run some focus groups among his potential clients. Through a process of informal networking he was soon able to find enough willing participants (local residents) to run two separate groups. He planned to conduct the sessions around a large dining room table in a nearby motel, where people would be able to help themselves to plenty of coffee and sandwiches. Each session was scheduled to last for two hours and Graham prepared for them carefully by compiling a list of the topics he wanted to discuss. In order to ensure he wouldn't forget what was said, Graham planned to record the discussions on tape.

When running a focus group the main points to remember are: run it on neutral territory; provide refreshments; use a pre-prepared 'discussion guide' which will encourage everyone to talk; use as many 'visuals' (such as photographs, drawings or mock-ups) as you can to stimulate people's thinking; record the session; and thank everyone with a small gift afterwards. It's also good practice to run at least two separate focus group sessions in order to compare and contrast the patterns of responses and information obtained.

24 Run an online focus group

An online focus group involves organising a 'virtual' meeting between three or four participants, in a chat room environment, for the purpose or prompting an open discussion about their ideas, thoughts and opinions relating to a specific marketing problem or opportunity area. This approach is particularly useful for bringing together participants who are extremely busy (say, business executives who would not be able to spare the time to meet you in person) and/or those who are located over a wide geographic area (where the time and costs of travelling would be prohibitive). In addition, it's an approach that costs virtually nothing—if you'll pardon the pun. Furthermore, with an online focus group, there's no need to worry about taking notes or having to use a tape recorder to capture the information gained because everyone's comments are automatically stored in written form and can easily be printed out at the touch of a button.

As with the more traditional focus group which takes place 'in person', you must select your online focus group participants carefully so that they reflect the composition of your intended (or actual) target market. Similarly, one of the keys to running an effective online focus group is the use of a well thought out and appropriate discussion guide. This should take the form of a list of pre-prepared open questions which you can feed into the discussion as it unfolds, in order to keep it on track. Remember that in cyberspace you don't have the benefit of non-verbal communication, which makes it more important than ever that you are well prepared.

In setting up an online focus group, contact your intended participants by telephone in the first instance. Explain exactly what you would like them to do and how the session would work. In particular, find out what time of day would be most convenient for them to take part. (This is especially important if one or more of them are located in different time zones.) Then schedule a time slot that will be convenient to everyone. Once the session is over, be sure to send each of your participants a thank you card together with a small token of your appreciation for having taken part.

25 Conduct a postal survey

When you need to find out a lot of facts and figures about a little known market, the traditional postal questionnaire survey comes into its own. Yes, the good old postal survey still has its place as a modern market research tool, despite the existence of the Internet! For one thing, not everyone is contactable by email, but they are by post. For another, there's a lot to be said for a 'tactile' medium that affords total confidentiality as well as the opportunity for respondents to ponder their responses in their own time. In carrying out a postal survey, there are three interrelated areas upon which to focus your attention. Let's take a brief look at each one:

WRITING A COVERING LETTER AND CONSTRUCTING THE QUESTIONNAIRE

A good covering letter is personalised to the target recipient; explains the background to the research; requests completion by a certain date; provides an incentive of some kind to participate; guarantees confidentiality; says 'thanks' in anticipation of a response; and is signed in ink by you as the sender. With regard to the questionnaire itself, make sure it is smartly presented, concise and easy to follow, and with instructions showing how to answer.

Order the questions so that the easy questions come first, followed by the main body of questions, with the most sensitive or 'private' questions concluding the questionnaire. A good tip which greatly simplifies the task of data analysis is to ask only closed, fully pre-coded questions (such as yes/no, multi-choice or rating scale style) which require the respondent to tick the answer which most closely resembles theirs. In addition, be sure to pilot test the questionnaire with a friend before mailing it out, to check that all your questions are unbiased and easy to understand. Also bear in mind that, in order to maximise response rates, you'll need to enclose a postage-paid return envelope.

SELECTING A SAMPLE OF NAMES AND ADDRESSES

Unless the population of individuals/companies that forms the subject of your study is small enough to enable everyone to be surveyed (known as a census), then you'll need to select a sample. This is a representative subset of the full population, from which you can draw conclusions about that population. As a general rule, you should aim to sample as many people as it takes to end up with between 50 and 100 fully completed questionnaires. Sampling is a two-step process:

- *Search for a 'sampling frame'—a list of the names and addresses of the full population of individuals/companies under investigation, such as you'd find in a telephone book or a business directory.*

- *Choose a sampling method (probability or non-probability) and select your sample.*

Providing a sampling frame is available then you should select your sample from it using an accepted random sampling procedure. This method is otherwise known as probability sampling, because it allows you to apply statistical probability theory when analysing your results, enabling you to calculate levels of confidence and limits of accuracy. If, however, no sampling frame is available (or affordable) then you'll need to put together the best sample you can find from a variety of sources which are conveniently at hand. This method is otherwise known as non-probability sampling, because such samples are, in theory, not necessarily representative of the full population which means that, strictly speaking, accuracy levels cannot be calculated. However, unless you have good reason to believe a convenience-based sample is likely to be unrepresentative, don't worry. It's still well worth going ahead because, in the end, the only person you have to convince about the accuracy of your findings is yourself.

ANALYSING THE RESULTS

Providing your questionnaire is made up of tick-the-box style questions, then the responses given can be added up easily and then interpreted in the form of simple frequency counts, percentages, averages and so on. If necessary, you can also go on to compare these types of basic statistics across different categories of respondent, such as male or female, or different types of company. Such analyses can be done by hand, but obviously it's a lot easier by computer.

26 Conduct an online survey

An online survey is almost identical to a postal survey except that everything is done electronically. This means it's ultra-fast, ultra-cheap and, since most businesses are on the Internet, it's ideal for conducting business-to-business research. However, its unique advantages make it especially useful if you want to do a large-scale survey in another country. Although there are a number of ways and means by which you can organise an online questionnaire, I'd like to tell you about a particular approach that will maximise your chances of getting a decent response rate—something that is notoriously difficult to do on the Internet. Here's an example showing what to do:

Only six months after launching a brand new type of specialised building product, the small company that developed it was enjoying so much success that the owners, Steve and Jeff, were already considering their options for expanding into new markets overseas. To investigate these marketing opportunities, a large-scale online questionnaire survey was carried out as follows:

Since the customers for their new product were mainly commercial architects, the first step was to purchase a list of email addresses for all those architects operating in their preferred overseas markets. The next step was to send a short email message to each one. In the email, Steve and Jeff introduced themselves and respectfully invited recipients to take part in their forthcoming questionnaire survey, briefly explaining what it would be about and how it would be administered, and offering a free summary of the main findings as an incentive to participate. Most importantly, the email also pointed out that the questionnaire would only take about 10 minutes to complete, and that all replies would be treated with the utmost confidentiality. To their delight, within a few days, and after a reminder email had been sent to all those who didn't respond within the first 24 hours, some 50 per cent replied to say they would take part. At this point, however, came the really clever bit. Rather than sending off the questionnaire as an attachment, Steve and Jeff simply emailed a thank you note requesting that the questionnaire be completed by a certain date, together with a 'click here' hyperlink connecting each respondent with a web site that hosted their questionnaire. This meant that when they came to analyse the responses, thanks to the power of automation the full range of statistics summarising the answers given by all respondents could be instantly accessed at the touch of a button. What's more, the computer was able to identify all those who had taken part and to whom a thank you letter was to be sent together with a copy of the summary of findings, as had been promised. Now that's computer power!

As you can see, the key to achieving a decent response rate is asking for a respondent's permission first, before sending the questionnaire. Moreover, the beauty of an online questionnaire is that, providing you set it up correctly on the web, it effectively eliminates the time and complexities involved in data analysis. What's more, the low cost-per-contact rate means it offers plenty of scope for sending out lots of reminder letters and follow-up thank you letters.

27 Interview by telephone

For a quick, convenient and comparatively inexpensive method of generating research information direct from customers, it's difficult to beat the telephone. Interviewing this way is particularly useful if you need to talk to people who are located over a wide geographic area, and when the questions you want to ask are relatively straightforward. In short, telephone interviewing is probably the quickest way of getting a 'feel' for people's opinions in a market. Here are the how-to-do-its.

A well designed questionnaire is the cornerstone of an effective telephone interviewing program, because it helps you to come across in a professional manner and ensures consistency in both the wording and sequencing of the questions you ask. Include only closed-ended (yes/no or multi-choice) questions, because it's so much easier to analyse the responses given to these types of questions than it is to analyse the answers given to open-ended questions. Indeed, a useful tip is to prepare your questionnaire so it can be reduced by photocopier onto a single sheet of paper and in such a way that you can record the answers given during each interview by ticking boxes, as appropriate, next to each question. That way, when you've completed all your interviews, it's really easy to add up and summarise all your results on one master sheet. Above all, before starting your interview program, always pilot test your questionnaire to iron out any problems and to check that it doesn't take more than about 10 minutes to complete. Anything much longer than this and your interviewee will almost certainly lose concentration.

Another key aspect of designing a telephone interview program is deciding which and how many people to call. Obviously, as with all forms of survey, your aim is to collect data from a relatively small sample of customers whose views are likely to be reflective of any larger population. Hence it usually makes sense to select your sample randomly from the appropriate section(s) of a telephone directory or something similar. As a general rule, if you keep dialling until you've completed between, say, 50 and 100 interviews, that should easily suffice.

When making each call, remember your first task is to get to speak to the right person before going on to explain the purpose of your call and to request their cooperation. If necessary, reassure them that all their answers will be kept strictly confidential. Adopt a positive and courteous manner; never deviate from your questionnaire; and always record the answers given on the spot. At the end of the set interview, by all means take the time to probe for additional information if your interviewee seems keen to keep on chatting. It never hurts to get as much feedback as you possibly can from a customer!

28 Turn your research project into a student research project

When it comes to deciding who should actually be involved in conducting a market research project, most owner–managers automatically assume there are only two options: either to hire a specialist market research agency to do it for you, or to do it yourself. The trouble is, more often than not, neither option is ideally suited to the small business. On the one hand, a professional agency is typically going to be way too expensive. On the other hand, depending on the nature of the project, doing it yourself can be a daunting, if not overwhelming, prospect due to the time commitments and complexities involved.

However, there is a third option, and it's one I've seen work extremely well in many small businesses. In fact, I think this idea is so good I've used it myself in my own businesses on three separate occasions to date, and with great success every time. It's the simple idea of sponsoring one or more students to do some market research on your behalf. The good news is that you certainly won't find any shortage of students ready and willing to help. Most university and other tertiary level business studies or marketing courses require students to undertake some form of practical market research project. This means you can benefit from a knowledgeable and enthusiastic student with access to libraries, computers and other facilities, who is able to conduct the research for you under the auspices of a reputable educational establishment. Best of all, to 'sponsor' a student simply means agreeing to cover their expenses, so the research need only end up costing you about the same as if you'd done it yourself. Here's how to go about it.

Contact all the colleges, universities and business schools in your area and find out which ones specialise in running courses in marketing with a practical research component. Telephone the course directors and ask them to give you all the details. Most likely, you'll be required to send a letter outlining your research objectives which can then be circulated to prospective students and their academic supervisors as a means of 'advertising' it as a sponsorship opportunity. Next, with a bit of luck, you'll be inundated with enquires from interested students and typically, at this stage, it will then be up to you to interview them and select the best one(s).

On the basis of my previous experience in sponsoring student research projects, I believe there are three keys for ensuring all goes well. First, it's important to be crystal clear about your research objectives right from the outset. The more specific you can be about the precise nature of your research requirements, the more this will keep the student focused and the subsequent research program 'lean and mean'. Second, make sure you choose the best student! Needless to say some students will be better equipped than others to help, so always take your time in selecting a top quality student who has all the right credentials. Third, be prepared to take on the role of an external supervisor. The more guidance and encouragement you can give a student in carrying out your research project, the more you'll both get out of it.

29 Look into the future with a PEST analysis

Here's the fascinating story of Encyclopedia Britannica:

In 1990, Encyclopedia Britannica was a company with an enviable track record. It had a two-hundred-year-old history, a brand name which was recognised and respected the world over, and had just posted an extremely healthy end-of-year profit. Yet within two short years, its sales and profits had almost completely collapsed! As you've probably already guessed, the main reason for this dramatic decline in the company's fortunes was the CD-ROM. During the early 1990s, a new breed of encyclopedias on CD that run on a personal computer completely redefined the nature of the market. Unlike the bulky book volumes of *Encyclopedia Britannica*, the CDs included video clips, voice-overs and background music to present information in a modern, easily accessible and highly entertaining way. Encyclopedia Britannica simply missed the boat in a classic case of 'out with the old, in with the new'. Interestingly, it took until the mid-1990s before *Encyclopedia Britannica* eventually appeared on CD and was able to start recovering its lost ground.

What this example illustrates is that, in seeking to understand a market, you must always try to predict any wider environmental trends and their future impact on that market. Assuming you don't have a crystal ball handy, the best way to do this is to conduct a PEST analysis. The acronym itself is made up of the first letter of the four main areas upon which to focus your efforts, as follows:

P = Political environment
Examples include fiscal/monetary policies, environmental policies, industrial policies, etc.

E = Economic environment
Examples include inflation, interest rates and the employment situation, etc.

S = Social environment
Examples include lifestyles, consumer movements and demographic change, etc.

T = Technological environment
Examples include product/process innovations, substitutes and raw materials, etc.

As you can see, a PEST analysis comprises all those factors which, over a medium or longer timeframe, will act to re-shape both buyer and competition behaviour and which could therefore dramatically change the face of a marketplace. Here's how to conduct a PEST analysis. Gather together a small number of people who are knowledgeable about the marketplace. Start off by making it clear that your intention is to analyse all the key factors relating to the wider business environment for the purposes of anticipating any newly emerging marketing opportunities or threats. Next, go into brainstorming mode and identify all the variables that you think should be considered under each category heading, writing them out on a whiteboard or flip-chart for everyone to consider. Continue the session by discussing the scenarios that are most likely to unfold in the foreseeable future and, in particular, any strategic implications.

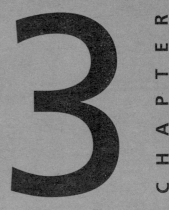

CHAPTER

3

IDEAS FOR FORMULATING A WINNING MARKETING STRATEGY

Formulating a winning marketing strategy involves the careful 'positioning' of a product or service in the marketplace so that it has a unique appeal to a certain group of target customers and is difficult for competitors to copy.

Owner–managers of successful small businesses do not pursue a strategy of trying to be 'all things to all people'. On the contrary, they define a target group of customers to whom they can make an irresistible offer.

Effective strategy is the pursuit of the right customers, with the right product or service, in the right way.

Identify your company's distinctive competencies

The key to successful marketing is to build a strategy around what you like doing and what you're good at. This means focusing on those things you do particularly well and making the most of them in the marketplace. Make a note of the following maxim:

A successful strategy is not based on doing what you like,
but liking what you do.

This is why it is important to clearly identify your company's actual or potential distinctive competencies. The term 'distinctive competencies' refers to those things your company is, or could be, particularly good at, such as your expertise areas, your know-how, skills and technologies. In fact, if you're reading this as someone who's already in business, then when you think about it, they're probably the very things which you built your business around and which are likely to have driven your success to date.

Assuming you're already in business, here are a few tips to help you identify your company's distinctive competencies. Start off by making a master list of all those tasks your company performs in the production and marketing areas of your business, and then make another list of all the underlying know-how, skills and technologies which enable you to perform those tasks. Next, create a shortlist by asking yourself which ones you do especially well and, in particular, highlighting those which you feel are truly distinctive in the sense that they are unique to your company. Finally, boil down your shortlist by crossing out those which are relatively easy for other companies to copy, imitate or acquire in some way, and it is highly likely that those remaining on the list are truly representative of your company's distinctive competencies.

By the way, once you've identified exactly what they are, make sure that from now on you never forget them! In order for them to remain as true leverage points around which to compete in future, you'll need to pay constant attention to maintaining and enhancing your company's abilities in these areas.

Make the most of your company's marketing assets

Another foundation stone of effective strategy development is always to choose to compete in such a way that you make the most of your 'marketing assets'. A marketing asset may be defined as anything your company already has, tangible or intangible, which differentiates its products or services in the minds of actual or potential customers. Unlike the assets which appear on your company balance sheet (and which are defined from an accountant's perspective), a marketing asset is not likely to have been assigned a dollar value in this way. Yet they can be of infinitely more value to the business than many of those items that do have a dollar value! For example, a few years ago, when the Rowntree confectionery company was bought out by the Nestlé group, the purchase price was around six times the company's book value. This was because Nestlé was not really interested in buying the company's manufacturing resources and other tangible assets; what they really wanted was to own the well known brand names of Kit Kat, Rolo and others in the Rowntree product line. In other words, Nestlé wanted to acquire a piece of the customer's mind—the company's 'hidden' marketing assets.

More often than not, a company's marketing assets are not immediately obvious, and you'll probably need to think long and hard (adopting a customer perspective) in order to identify them. Here are a few examples to get you thinking:

A reputable company name. Even though you might be a very small company, if you have a reputable company name, then no matter how modest you think it is (such as a reputation for integrity or dependability), this is a distinctive asset to be exploited in your choice of strategy.

An experienced and knowledgeable sales team. Some companies are highly dependent on the reputation of their salespeople as being knowledgeable and experienced experts in their field. Under these circumstances, salespeople should be seen as valuable marketing assets upon which to build a winning strategy in the marketplace.

A 'local' location. Many small companies operate on a local basis only, and yet still find themselves having to compete with large nationwide operators. In some markets, however, a 'local' location can be a powerful marketing asset. For example, a locally owned and operated pie-maker competing with a national food company could maximise the advantage of being local by baking traditional pies 'like granny used to make' and creating a strong regional identity for their brand.

A well known and highly respected owner–manager. Some companies are run by individuals who are well known and highly respected public figures. This could be for all manner of reasons. For example, they may have been involved in the industry for a long time, or might have achieved some measure of fame in an earlier career. These people naturally attract public attention and as such might well represent an important source of competitive advantage.

32 Analyse and segment the market

Here's an example that clearly demonstrates the benefits of analysing and segmenting the market:

Some time ago, a French winemaker was considering relocating to Australia so his new wife could be nearer to her family. Before making the move, however, he decided to commission a marketing consultant to analyse the Australian wine market. The consultant subsequently provided him with a detailed report that suggested the market could be broken down into four main segments. Here's a brief summary of his analysis:

Segment 1—the connoisseurs. This segment comprised some 5 per cent of all wine drinkers and was a market which was in very slow decline. These people were typically older (often retired) and seriously wealthy. They were extremely enthusiastic and knowledgeable about wine, had their own wine cellars, and usually bought their wines privately through wine merchants. They had a preference for aged, top quality French and European wines.

Segment 2—the brand seekers. This segment made up some 20 per cent of all wine drinkers and was a market which had grown steadily for some time. These people were typically over 35 years old, on a good salary and were highly 'image conscious'. While being quite serious about their wine, with well stocked wine racks, they were also quite conservative and tended to stick loyally with certain brand names. In particular they tended to be supportive of home grown 'boutique' labels, usually purchased through their local wine shop.

Segment 3—the adventurers. This segment comprised approximately 25 per cent of the market, but had been declining steadily for a number of years. These customers were typically young and upwardly mobile (yuppies), with plenty of disposable income and would buy wine of any type from anywhere, and from the middle to upper price bracket. These wine drinkers would always be keen to learn more by trying a new wine. Indeed, as their tastes matured, many of them would turn into 'brand seekers' by the time they reached middle age.

Segment 4—the price takers. This segment made up the bulk of the market, representing some 50 per cent of all wine drinkers. It was a market that had remained constant for quite some time and included people of all ages from the lower to middle income range. They knew very little about wine and would usually buy 'any half-decent plonk' as long as it was cheap enough, straight off the supermarket shelf.

Thanks to the marketing consultant's insightful analysis, the French winemaker was able to make an informed judgement about if and how he would be able to compete in the Australian wine market. Indeed, upon further investigation, a decision was made to enter the market with a well branded quality wine aimed primarily at the 'brand seekers' segment, and sold on the basis of building strong relationships with selected wine shops and a promotional campaign featuring Australian wine experts.

As you can see from this example, segmentation involves the subdivision of a larger market into smaller groups of customers with similar needs and wants and responsiveness to marketing offerings. It thereby enables you to isolate a specific target market that your company is best able to serve. In attempting to segment the market there are many possible criteria which could be chosen, but typically they relate to one (or more) of the following basic categories:

- *geographics (where customers are), such as whether they're local, regional or national*

- *demographics (who customers are), such as their age, sex and so on*

- *psychographics (how customers think), such as their beliefs and attitudes*

It is important to appreciate, however, that any variable can be used as a basis for segmentation, providing customers within the resulting segments have similar needs and wants and the segments are large and profitable enough to justify being targeted. Indeed, the greater your ability to segment a market in new and creative ways, the more likely it is that you will find a way to exploit it to your greatest advantage.

33 Find the right target market

Once market segments have been identified, the decision about which customer group to target will be crucial to your success. Obviously different market segments will be attractive to you for different reasons, so it is important that you make your choice carefully and on the basis of as much information as possible. Generally speaking, however, a segment will be more attractive if it scores highly across a number of key questions, as follows:

Do you have the necessary skills and resources to be able to compete? Only choose to compete in a market where you can gain maximum 'leverage' from your existing company strengths: your skills, knowledge, expertise, competencies and marketing assets. Always play to your strengths.

Is the market big enough to be profitable? Ideally, you should choose to compete in a small market segment or 'niche' that you can dominate (a market niche is a corner of a market that is so small that it is not actively pursued by other firms). However, make sure the niche isn't going to be so small as to be unprofitable. While you should certainly be looking for a gap in the market, you will also need to make sure there's a market in the gap! Notably, the best markets are small ones but with plenty of projected growth.

Is the market too competitive? Obviously a market with lots of competitors jostling for business isn't a very attractive one, and especially if there are large, well established players in the field. Nor is a market attractive that would be easy for new competitors to enter should they see you doing well. Examples of markets that other companies would find difficult to enter are almost always those which require a company to possess certain skills, specialist knowledge or technologies in order for them to be able to compete effectively.

Are you able to offer something different? An attractive market segment is one where your company will be able to offer customers something unique, something that they will really need and/or want, and something they will value. In other words, a market in which you will be able to enjoy a clear competitive advantage.

34 Focus and concentrate your company's marketing effort

Numerous academic studies have set out to determine the key ingredients of a winning marketing strategy for the smaller business. Without exception, these studies have highlighted the need to focus and concentrate the small firm's limited resources onto a narrowly defined target market segment. For example, one such study carried out in the United States by Clifford and Cavanagh concluded:

> *High growth companies succeed by identifying and meeting the needs of certain kinds of customers, not all customers, for special kinds of products and services, not all products and services. Business academics call this market segmentation. Entrepreneurs call it common sense.*

The point is, one of the defining characteristics of any small business is that it has extremely limited resources. This means that no small business will ever have sufficient means to be able to serve a large market, in its entirety, equally as well as a big company. If it attempts to do so it will inevitably end up spreading its resources so thinly as to be unable to compete effectively. For example, it will always have fewer salespeople, less money to spend on advertising and promotion, less to spend on product development and so on.

The key to success is to make the most of your limited resources by focusing and concentrating them on a well defined group of target customers. Just as the 'jack of all trades and master of none' rarely becomes a wealthy individual, the evidence shows that for small businesses it is just the same.

35 Become a market rule-maker, not a rule-taker

A question I'm often asked is: 'How do you know a good strategy from a bad one?' Well what is *not* a good strategy is to offer what everyone else does—a similar product or service at a similar price, and in a similar way, to a similar group of target customers—because your profit margins will always get squeezed by the bigger players who can undercut your prices. On the contrary, the key to successful strategy is *not* to blindly accept the world as everyone else sees it and play the marketing game according to the same rules as your competitors. The real trick is to try and out-manoeuvre the competition by changing the rules of the game to your advantage. In other words, you should aim to become a rule-maker in the market, rather than being yet another rule-taker. Here are three of the best ways to become a market rule-maker:

1 You could change the method of doing business in some basic way.
For example, a small provincial bank took the banking market by storm
when it was the first bank to launch an Internet banking service. Since all
its customers' transactions were conducted through the Internet, it had no
branches; which meant it was cheaper to run as well as being more
convenient for customers.

2 You could redefine traditional market boundaries. For example, a few
years ago a small chain of jewellery stores redefined the traditional concept
of the 'up-scale retail jewellery store' when they launched a nationwide
network of self-service style stores selling a range of less expensive
'costume' jewellery, thereby attracting a new and previously untapped
market.

3 You could create an entirely new market from scratch. For example, by
launching an altogether new product, in much the same way as Steve Jobs
did when he launched the Apple computer, which was the world's first
desktop personal computer.

36 Apply the formula S = HVTC + LCTY

This is a magical little success formula to help you develop a winning
marketing strategy. Here's what the letters stand for:

Success = Higher Value to Customer + Lower Cost to You

It's a useful formula because it reminds us that one of the keys to
developing a successful strategy is to try and find something else—
something new and different that we can offer our customers that's of high
value to them, in the sense that it'll help to better satisfy their needs and
wants. Ideally, however, it should be something that we can offer at a
lower cost compared with our competitors.

Obviously, if you can put this equation to work, not only will you be
differentiating your offer from those of your competitors in the
marketplace, and in a way that's meaningful to your customers, but you'll
also be doing so in a way that makes it difficult for your competitors to
copy because of the higher costs involved to them. Try to apply this
common sense little formula, and you won't go far wrong!

37 Clearly define your competitive advantage

Let's make no mistake about it, the creation of a competitive advantage is at the very heart of marketing strategy formulation. In a nutshell, this means deciding exactly how you're going to compete in the marketplace. A competitive advantage may be defined as:

> A *unique benefit, or combination of benefits, which in the eyes of target customers makes a product or service stand out as superior to its competitors in the marketplace.*

Here's an example of how one small business developed their competitive advantage:

> When a small printing company decided to redefine its market and focus on providing members of the legal profession with an ultra-fast, high precision printing service, it shifted the emphasis away from having to compete on price. Since the two brothers who owned the company had degrees in Law and English respectively, they were able to use their combined expertise to provide a specialist service for anyone requiring an error free, legally binding document, contract, share issue prospectus or similar documentation. As you can see, these brothers did everything right. They focused and concentrated their resources on a well defined target market and played to their strengths. In doing so, they created for themselves a clear competitive advantage in the marketplace and, as a result, profits soared. Here's an extract from their strategy statement:
>
> *Our target customers will be members of the legal profession. Our competitive advantage will be to offer a fast, 'one-stop print shop' to these customers. In addition to typesetting and printing, we will specialise in the formatting and writing of all legal documentation, including legal and technical advice, a guarantee of error free results, and an on-time every time delivery service.*

When developing a competitive advantage, the essential factors are twofold. First, always compete by delivering products and services that provide a superior value to customers rather than ones that simply cost less. For example, products which are of a higher quality and/or which deliver greater benefits to the customer, and/or services which are faster or better in some way. The second essential factor is that it should be 'defensible'. In other words, it should utilise a skill or some other resource of your company that competitors will find hard to copy. A defensible competitive advantage can be created out of any of your company's strengths or distinctive competencies relative to the competition.

Once you have decided upon the precise nature of your company's intended competitive advantage, you should write it down in the form of a detailed strategy statement. This is a succinct outline of all the key aspects of your strategy, including your choice of target market, competitive advantage and the main features of your offer to the customer. A well written strategy statement acts as a reference point and gives a clear lead for all subsequent operating decisions.

38 Sell only what customers need and want

Marketing folklore has it that a leading food manufacturer once launched a new dog food called 'Top Dog'. A new pet foods division of the company was formed, and Top Dog was planned to be the flagship product of what would become a range of pet foods to be distributed nationwide. Unfortunately, however, things did not go according to plan. In the first six months, despite a huge TV advertising and promotional blitz, Top Dog sales were extremely disappointing. The company directors couldn't understand what could have gone wrong because the product was manufactured to the highest quality standards, the promotional campaign was second to none, and the 100-strong sales force was composed of highly trained professionals. So in an effort to turn the situation around, the entire sales force was gathered together for a special sales convention at a plush hotel. The sales director was determined to raise the spirits of his beleaguered sales team and started his address with a motivating speech, followed by the classic 'call and response' approach that went something like this:

> 'So what's the name of the world's finest quality dog food?'
> 'Top Dog!' (came a somewhat restrained response from his audience)
> 'And who's got the number one advertising campaign?'
> 'Top Dog!'
> 'And who's got the biggest distribution network?'
> 'Top Dog!
> 'And who's got the best salespeople?'
> 'Top Dog!'
> 'And who's got the most attractive package for the retailer?'
> 'TOP DOG!'

Sensing a distinct lack of enthusiasm among his troops, the sales director cut to the chase.

'Okay then, so why the heck aren't we selling more product?' he asked.

The auditorium became hushed, until one brave soul finally shouted out the reply that said it all.

'The product isn't selling because the dogs don't like it!'

Obviously, at the core of your marketing strategy is your choice of product or service to sell, but if your target customers don't need or want what you have to offer, then no amount of money, salespeople or clever advertising can save you from certain disaster. How good is your product or service?

39 Set longer and shorter term marketing objectives

Objective setting is probably one of the most misunderstood aspects of marketing, so here's a quick summary of what's involved.

First, let's be crystal clear about what is meant by an objective and how it differs from a strategy. Basically, a marketing objective should specify *what* you want to achieve over a specific time period, whereas a marketing strategy should define exactly *how* you intend to go about achieving your objectives.

Second, let's be equally clear about the kind of objectives that need to be set. They should always cover not only what outputs you want to achieve (such as a certain number of unit sales or a certain number of responses to a promotional campaign), but also the cost input levels you are willing to incur in the process. There's little point in setting out to achieve something at any cost!

Third, and most importantly, be sure to differentiate between your longer term 'strategic' objectives and your shorter term 'tactical' objectives. Strategic objectives relate to what you want a particular product or service to achieve over a time horizon of, say, 12 months. By contrast, tactical objectives relate to a range of activities to be achieved over a series of much shorter time horizons of, say, four-weekly periods, and all of which should add up to enable your strategic objectives to be realised by the end of the year. This means that strategic objectives need only be stated in terms of basic sales and profit targets. Shorter term objectives, on the other hand, need to be much more detailed in nature. In effect, they are the working objectives that apply to individual members of staff (or teams) when performing their day-to-day duties. For example, salespeople might have specific sales objectives by customer or by territory. Customer service people might have objectives relating to service response times or customer relationship-building activities, and marketing managers might have advertising and promotional targets, among others.

40 Always do your sums

No matter how brilliant your new marketing strategy may appear to be, it is imperative that you check to make sure it's going to be financially viable before going ahead. Basically, there are three sets of calculations to make: a break-even analysis, a cash flow forecast and a budgeted profit and loss account. Let's take a closer look at each:

> A break-even analysis. This is where you set out the simple arithmetic explaining how you will cover the costs of your proposed strategy. Your aim is to estimate two things: exactly what it will cost to produce and deliver the product or service, in terms of both the fixed and variable costs involved; and then how many unit sales you need to make, at a given selling price, before you have covered your costs and start making a profit. This is your break-even point.

> A cash flow forecast. It is essential to be aware of the cash flow implications of your proposed strategy and not just the profit implications. In fact, conducting a cash flow forecast is arguably the most vital piece of financial planning of all. I'm sure you will already have come across many small businesses that went 'belly up', not because they weren't making a profit, but because they became cash starved and couldn't keep going. Here's a good way to think about the difference between profit and cash:

> Profit is a concept but cash is a fact!

> A good cash flow forecast is a month-by-month or even a weekly chart showing exactly how much money will be coming into the business and how much will be going out of it. This means you will be able to determine if, when, and how much additional finance you may need in order to pursue a particular strategy.

> A budgeted profit and loss account. In effect, this is an 'at a glance' summary of just how successful you think you will be after one year of trading. It shows your projected sales figure, details all your fixed and variable costs, and highlights your bottom line profit or loss figure. It should

also include any adjustments you need to make in order to account for depreciation, or any special tax allowances that might apply in your particular case.

Although all three of these calculations can be made by hand, it is better to use an accounting spreadsheet package on a personal computer. The computer makes it easy to compare different sets of calculations based on different sales forecasts, selling prices and other cost related variables. It's always advisable to consider 'best' and 'worst' case scenarios. If your figures are acceptable across the full spectrum of possibilities, then you'll be giving yourself the best chance of success.

⁴¹ Think until it hurts!

Here's an abbreviated version of a passage from another of my favourite books, *Marketing Warfare* by Al Ries and Jack Trout:

Marketing wars are fought in a mean and ugly place. A terrain that's tricky and difficult to understand. They are fought inside the mind. It is a totally intellectual war, in which you try to out-manoeuvre your competitors on a battleground that nobody has ever seen because it can only ever be imagined in the mind.

Let's not kid ourselves, marketing strategy formulation is not easy. In fact, in my experience, making sense of a marketplace and coming up with the 'right' strategy is so difficult that it makes your brain hurt! Not only does it demand an ability to think analytically, in the sense that you need to be able to research and interpret market facts and figures, but perhaps even more importantly it also demands an ability to think conceptually, creatively and imaginatively. As Ries and Trout so eloquently remind us, deciding how to segment a market and formulate a winning strategy is fundamentally an intellectual challenge of the highest order. This means that when formulating your strategy, it is wise to seek the advice and opinions of as many people as possible, especially those who are knowledgeable about the marketplace. Above all, however, be prepared to think until it hurts and then, if necessary, to think some more!

4

IDEAS FOR PROVIDING BETTER COMPANY INFORMATION MATERIALS

The term 'information materials' refers to all standard letters, brochures, leaflets, booklets, information packs, web sites and other methods of disseminating company information as an aid to the sales process.

Owner–managers of successful small businesses realise that these kinds of materials present a real opportunity to stand out from the competition and be noticed.

Creating outstanding
company information
materials is the art of doing
a common thing in an
uncommon way.

42 Animate your sales brochure

The five senses by which we all communicate with the world are sight, sound, touch, smell and taste, and the more of them we can use to help sell our products and services, the better; because they get the customer involved with what we have to offer. So why on earth don't we appeal to more than one of the senses when designing our sales brochures? Why do we persist in distributing 'standard' brochures that are more or less the same as everyone else's, and especially when our product or service is the kind that lends itself to being presented in a more animated way? After all, there are plenty of 'involvement devices' that can easily be used to improve, if not completely transform, most sales brochures. In using these devices, the aim is to make your sales brochure really stand out by 'bringing your product or service to life' in the mind of a prospective customer. The main types of involvement devices to consider are as follows:

1 Product-based involvement devices enable prospects to feel, smell or taste a sample of your product. For example, the manufacturer of a new type of protective clothing could staple a small piece of the material to their brochure so that the customer's attention can be drawn to certain of its features and benefits whilst actually being able to feel the material between their fingers.

2 Media-based involvement devices encourage prospects to experience something related to the media itself. For example, pop-ups, see-throughs, concertina folds, pull-outs and so on. Of course, you don't have to be restricted to just paper, cellophane or cardboard. One of the most entertaining brochures I've seen was also a speaking brochure. By touching a 'press here' button, you could hear a short message from the company's managing director, personally delivering his company's customer service promise!

3 Print-based involvement devices involve prospects through the use of optical illusions, crossword puzzles, checklists, upside-down headlines and such like, but most importantly, through the use of 'action' photographs. Indeed, as an involvement device, you could say an action photograph really is worth a thousand words. For example, you could include a sequence of shots showing how your product works, maybe some 'before' and 'after' pictures or, better still, you could provide 'amazing but true' photographic evidence of a dramatic demonstration taking place.

By the way, if you're thinking that incorporating some of these ideas might prove to be a little on the expensive side, then you'd be right! A good brochure will certainly register more than just a blip on the radar scale of your business expenses. Nevertheless, ask yourself this: can you afford *not* to invest in a better and more distinctive sales brochure? After all, for many businesses it's the only 'shop window' they've got.

(43) Support your brochure with an audio tape

Here's an example of how Tom, a professional photographer, uses this idea to differentiate his information pack from those of his competitors. Picture the scene:

A young woman is planning her wedding. Unsure as to which photographer to book for the big day, she picks up the telephone and requests an information pack from four photographers who have advertised their services in the local directory. Sure enough, a couple of days later all four information packs arrive in the morning mail. Predictably, all four envelopes contain a colour brochure, but to the young woman's surprise, one of them also includes an audio tape. Intrigued to find out what's on the tape, she puts the brochures to one side (after all, they all look much the same) and decides to listen to the tape in her car on the way to work that morning. As the tape begins to play, it goes something like this:

Against the background sounds of people cheering and wedding bells ringing, Jack and Dorothy, who have been happily married for 25 years, reminisce about their wedding day. It soon becomes clear that they are looking through their old wedding photo album and, as they do, they go on to tell the listener how thankful they are that they chose Tom to take the photos that day, and what a professional job he did. After a few minutes their voices fade away as another couple, this time married for 10 years, tell a similar story. Next, another couple who have only been married for a few months give their testimonial, once again waxing lyrical about Tom's services. A few moments later, and now towards the end of the tape, Tom himself does the voiceover. He thanks the listener for their inquiry and explains how the next step is to telephone him to arrange for a free, no obligation consultation and quotaton. Finally, he encourages his listeners to act NOW by explaining that if they return the audio tape at the time of the consultation, they'll get a free copy of his booklet *The Wedding Planner*, a step-by-step guide to planning the perfect wedding.

As you can see, an audio tape can be an effective means of communicating information about your products and services. It can be used either alongside or instead of your existing sales brochure. Adding the fresh new dimension of sound differentiates your information from that of your competitors, and also serves to communicate your sales message in a uniquely personal way, especially when your own voice features on the tape.

To make the most of this kind of media, an intimate style that really sells your product or service in a very personal way works best. Like a well designed advertisement, start off by aiming to get the prospect's attention, then build interest and the desire to buy. Finally, ask for some form of action by providing an incentive for your prospect to contact you. You might even be able to do this in a way that encourages prospects to return the tapes. Notably, it is always a good idea to use verbal testimonials from satisfied customers. In addition, you could quote some figures or statistics that will further substantiate your claims and add the reassurance factor. If you already have a recognisable theme music or jingle that forms part of your radio advertising, then you can use it to great effect as introductory or background music on your tape. Otherwise, simply use any kind of background sound that helps to create the right atmosphere for your sales message by stimulating your listener's imagination.

44 Computerise your product information

If you sell products of a technical nature, then making your product information available to customers in the form of a computer disk may well be a sensible option. Of course, the beauty of this approach is that a computer disk can provide much more information than a glossy brochure and yet, at the same time, it's far cheaper to produce and easier to update. Here's an example of this idea in action:

Jim is one of those people who really gets enthusiastic about the type of car he drives and his is a Buick, which he bought from his local dealer. Recently, as part of a campaign to promote the latest range of Buicks, Jim received a computer disk from his dealer. As you can imagine, the disk enabled him to interrogate a vast database of detailed information about each new model in the range, from technical specifications to performance figures and prices. What a great way to attract him back into the dealer's for a test drive!

When putting your product information on disk, make it as interactive as possible, allowing prospects to key-in their specific requirements in such a way as to help them through their decision-making process by providing instant feedback and buying recommendations. Once you've got your product information on disk you can either use it instead of, or as a part of, your standard information pack. Alternatively, you could arm your salespeople with one as a means of helping them to make the sale or, if it's appropriate, you could even use it as a stand alone 'sales robot' in your showroom.

45 Enclose a company biography with your information pack

Is there an interesting story to tell about how you and your staff have had to battle heroically in the face of adversity and against all the odds to build your business? If so, then you should consider taking advantage of it by telling your story in the form of a 'company biography'.

When an inquirer requests that you send an information pack, a company biography is something else to include. It's a typed one or two page narrative which simply celebrates the story behind your company and its products and services. It doesn't attempt to sell, nor does it attempt to inform the reader about anything that's even remotely relevant to their purchase decision. Rather, its sole purpose is entertainment value. It's something different that an inquirer wouldn't normally expect to receive in an information pack. Perhaps something they might enjoy reading over a cup of coffee, for no other reason than just because it's a great story.

A company biography works best when it's written in the first person by you as the owner–manager of the business, and in a very personal way. Be sure to include the word 'story' in your title, so it's obvious what it is, followed by your name as the author. For example:

'The Story Behind ABC Ltd' by John Smith
or
'ABC Ltd: Our Story' by John Smith

Print it straight off your computer on plain paper and in black and white. There's no need to use colour or to design it in any special way because, by keeping it simple and deliberately not attempting to attract attention to it, it's far more likely to succeed in doing just that. With regard to the content of your company biography, aim to maximise the human interest angle. Start your story at the beginning, that is to say the moment when, in true entrepreneurial style, you had your first flash of inspiration or 'vision' of what you wanted to achieve. Then go on to unfold the story of your journey towards making it happen, building your business into what it is today. Above all, be sure to highlight all the twists and turns, and especially all the highs and lows that you and your staff have endured along the way. Evidence of an enterprising spirit, ingenuity, sacrifice, hard work and a never-say-die attitude are all the ingredients of a compelling company biography that's guaranteed to capture a prospective customer's imagination, and leave them more inclined to want to do business with you in preference to anyone else.

46 Enclose a supplier evaluation check with your information pack

A 'supplier evaluation check' outlines all the key information that any professional buyer is going to need in order to evaluate your company as a potential supplier. This is not sales information, but purely background information about your company itself. By including one of these whenever a professional buyer requests an information pack, the probability of making it onto their shortlist increases because the purpose of a supplier evaluation check is to help the buyer to do their job.

In putting together your supplier evaluation check, cover all the basic company information your buyer is going to need. For example, start with your company's name, address and its registered office, before moving on to give details of your number of employees, your facilities and equipment, your quality standards, memberships with professional bodies and so on. The information should be presented so it can be read at a glance and should be short, sharp and straight to the point. Most importantly, it should be purely factual so that, in effect, you have simply profiled your company's 'identity'. As long as it does not attempt to sell, it will be the perfect complement to your existing sales literature.

47 Provide staff profiles

Firms that offer highly specialised professional services, such as architects or lawyers, often fail to fully appreciate exactly what is important to customers when making a purchase decision. Sure, it's true that to a considerable extent their customers are buying a firm's reputable name and, yes, they might even be influenced more than a little by a prestigious sounding address and smart premises. However, what they are really buying is the knowledge, expertise and experience of the individual staff member or members who will be primarily responsible for designing their house or arguing their case in court. That's why I always recommend that, when selling professional services, one of the most important types of information materials to hand out to prospective customers, or to include in a company information pack, is staff profile sheets. In effect, staff profile sheets focus exclusively on selling your people individually. In fact, just as an employer would want to see a fully detailed curriculum vitae for each job applicant before hiring a new recruit, so too would a prospective customer use a staff profile sheet to make it easy to evaluate the quality of your company's staff before making their purchase decision.

It usually makes sense to have a separate profile sheet for each staff member because this means you can distribute them selectively, whilst at the same time making it easier for them to be updated as and when it becomes necessary. When designing a staff profile sheet it is important to personalise it as much as possible by including a portrait-style photograph of each staff member, together with a few personal details such as their marital status and their hobbies and interests. This gives your staff a 'human face'. Next, go on to give details of their career history. As a general rule, a good structure to adopt is to provide information under the following headings:

- *Previous positions*
- *Academic and professional qualifications*
- *Membership of professional bodies*
- *Career highlights and key achievements to date*
- *Current job title, responsibilities, and specialist areas of expertise*

48 Try the alternative quotation technique

I was once invited to facilitate a series of brainstorming sessions for a group of local businesspeople. Once a week we would all meet up to brainstorm a particular business problem that one or other of the group was experiencing, with the intention of coming up with some innovative solutions. Here's an outline of one of the many problems we addressed, and for which we were able to find a solution that proved to work remarkably well:

John, the owner of a mid-sized firm of commercial painters and decorators, was particularly proud of his company's reputation for delivering an exceptionally high standard of workmanship. His staff were all highly trained tradespeople, they always used top quality materials and their standard of finish was second to none. However, over recent months John was concerned to see that, although his firm was being asked to quote on an increasing number of jobs, as a proportion of the total, fewer and fewer contracts were actually being won. Hence, the question he posed to our brainstorming group went something like this:

'When a prospective customer asks for a formal written quote on a particular piece of business, how do you stop it from being thrown straight in the waste bin by those buyers who only ever seem to make decisions purely on the basis of comparing the bottom line prices of the quotes they receive ... the short-sighted ones who seem oblivious to the superior value for money that a higher priced quote might represent?'

Well this is a classic problem for any company selling customised services at the top end of the market. However, we did come up with a solution. By sending an 'alternative quotation' that literally gives the buyer the choice between two alternative offers, you'll at least be drawing attention to what they won't get by buying cheaper, and in doing so, be giving yourself a better chance of making a sale. As you'll appreciate, the key to this idea is to give the prospect a stark choice between two very differently priced quotes. Whereas the first one should represent your standard price/package offer, the second should be a really budget deal at a rock bottom price. More to the point, you should deliberately contrast the precise specifications and benefits of each offer by putting them side by side on the same page and, most importantly, with the two different prices prominently featured on the bottom line. That way, they can be readily compared at a glance. You could even use a highlighter pen to clearly differentiate between the two offers in terms of what the customer would or would not get for their money. Of course, you may or may not be serious about your budget offer—that's up to you—but the point is that with this approach you'll at least have succeeded in making it crystal clear to the prospect that you only get what you pay for!

49 Consider a very simple web site

A web site may be defined as a company's address in cyberspace where people can pay an 'electronic visit' from anywhere around the world and, if required, download product information, catalogues or an order form.

There are many potential advantages associated with having your own web site. It creates a 'leading edge' company image, reaches online potential customers, can distribute your information around the world and allows instant updates of your information. However, it is important to be realistic about the role a web site should play in your business, because it is all too easy to spend far too much money on a sophisticated, fancy web site that doesn't pay for itself! In fact, I'd say that perhaps the most useful role it can play for most small businesses is simply that of another information source for both new and existing customers, but with the added advantage of including an email link for anyone wishing to place an order or talk to you further about your products and services. In other words, my advice is to keep it simple!

In designing your web site, make sure that your home page (the first page of your web site that users will see) is clean and easy to view. Include your company name, logo and perhaps your mission statement, together with a mini-menu that links the user to various pages. These pages could include your product catalogue, details of your service provision, staff profiles and the like. The main points to bear in mind regarding effective web site design are as follows:

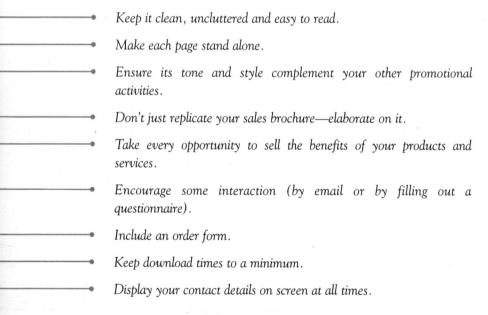

- *Keep it clean, uncluttered and easy to read.*

- *Make each page stand alone.*

- *Ensure its tone and style complement your other promotional activities.*

- *Don't just replicate your sales brochure—elaborate on it.*

- *Take every opportunity to sell the benefits of your products and services.*

- *Encourage some interaction (by email or by filling out a questionnaire).*

- *Include an order form.*

- *Keep download times to a minimum.*

- *Display your contact details on screen at all times.*

Having created your new web site, include the address on all your stationery, business cards and other handout and promotional materials.

In addition, you should list your web site with as many search engines as you can to make it as easy as possible for people to access. The only truly successful web sites are those that can be found easily.

50 Arm your salespeople with product checklists

If you're in retail, or indeed any business selling a wide range of interrelated products, this idea could easily be worth thousands of dollars of extra business. It's the simple idea of arming your salespeople with a series of product checklists as a means of helping customers think through the full extent of their purchasing requirements. Here is an example of how it works:

> Mrs Jones visits a DIY hardware store and picks up two large tins of white household paint. She eventually arrives at the sales counter and gets her purse out. At this point the salesperson enquires as to what sort of decorating work she is planning to do, and checks that she's bought the right kind of paint and enough to do the job. Before ringing the till, however, the salesperson then proceeds to say something like this:
>
> 'Mrs Jones, just to make sure you've got everything you're going to need to do the job, we've prepared this special checklist for home decorators—would it be helpful if I just quickly ran through it with you?'
>
> Mrs Jones doesn't want to be inconvenienced by getting home only to find out she's forgotten something, so she agrees to go through the checklist with the salesperson. It includes a number of items such as brushes, stepladders, sandpaper, rollers, cleaning cloths, masking tape, paint trays, overalls and so on.

As you can see, when using a product checklist in this way, it's highly likely there's going to be at least one or two items a customer hadn't thought of—and of course this is an extra sale that would otherwise have been missed. What's more, it's a great way to show that you are truly customer-focused in the way you run your business. With a little imagination, the product checklist idea can be adapted easily to suit all manner of selling situations to the mutual benefit of the customer and your business. In fact, there's no reason why you shouldn't arm your salespeople with a whole series of checklists, each of which relates to a different kind of customer need/product application.

51 Send out company postcards

Sending out a postcard-style 'company postcard' featuring a photograph of your staff, yourself, your product, your premises, your fleet of vehicles or even perhaps a humorous cartoon drawing of any of the above, can be an extremely useful method of communicating with your actual or prospective customers. For example, you could use it to confirm an appointment, as a thank you card, or as a giveaway. In particular, a postcard is an ideal way to follow up with a group of prospective customers you may have just met, say at a conference or trade exhibition, as a way of letting them know how much you enjoyed meeting them and that you'll be in contact soon. In designing your postcard, make sure it carries a sales message and some useful information about your company and/or its products and services, together with your contact details. Most importantly, however, when sending out a postcard always write it by hand. That way, your message will come across as novel, friendly and personal, which is exactly what everyone likes about receiving postcards!

52 Hand out better business cards

Business cards are probably the most widely used promotional tool of all. They give people a permanent record of your name and contact details, and make a statement about you and your company. So here are some of the main points to bear in mind when designing a good business card:

1 Decide on the mood, tone and style of your business card, and make sure that it's going to reflect the right company image.

2 Be sure to include any of your basic corporate identity requirements, such as your company colours, logo style and your slogan or tag line.

3 Avoid using a microscopic typeface that's too small to be easily read, and always print your main address and telephone number in bold so it stands out from your mobile number, fax number, email address and web site details.

4 Use the back of the card to communicate any other useful or important information, such as:

- *a list of your products and services*

- *a map showing your location*

- *your trading hours*

- *your key sales message*

- *your 'customer care' promise*

- *your company mission statement.*

5 If you provide a personal service, personalise your card by including a photograph of yourself.

6 Consider giving your card some novelty value to ensure it's memorable. For example:

- *Make it up with a magnetic strip so it can be used as a fridge magnet.*

- *Make it sticky-backed so it sticks to your products.*

- *Make it a musical business card or one that includes a 3-D image.*

53 Improve your letterhead

Think of all the times your customers see your company letterhead. Chances are they'll see it at least a couple of times during the early stages of their buying process when initial contact is made and when you're sending them information. Then they'll see it again when you're organising a sales demonstration, confirming their order details or arranging their installation and delivery. Then no doubt they'll see it yet again on any number of occasions when you're writing to keep in touch, doing repeat business or servicing them in some way. That's a lot of 'exposures', which is why it's important to make sure your letterhead is impressive to customers and, in particular, that it also works for you as a promotional tool.

Let's review the main ingredients of an effective letterhead. First, it must *look good*. In other words, visually, it must be well laid out on the page. There is a multitude of layouts ranging from the 'classic', traditional letterhead through to the more modern and funky 'designer' styles from which to choose, so be sure to select one which will best suit the nature of your products and services and your target customer requirements. By the way, it's always worth remembering that a good quality paper, and especially one that feels as good as it looks, can go a long way towards enhancing a customer's perceptions about the quality of your company's products and services. Second, it must *inform*. This is the basic function of any letterhead and requires that you clearly communicate your company's name/logo, address and contact details (in your usual 'house style' and colours) together with, if necessary, a listing of your company directors and a brief description of your product(s) and service(s). Third, it must *persuade*. This is a vital ingredient that's typically overlooked; yet all it takes is the inclusion of a brief sales message of some kind. This could be in the form of a list of benefits, a mission statement, a customer service promise or a slogan of business; it doesn't really matter just as long as you don't waste this valuable opportunity to tell your customers what's in it for them. In fact, it's so important that you might even consider putting it right across the top of the page! In effect, the humble letterhead provides you with some excellent advertising space, so ask yourself—are you making the most of it?

5

IDEAS FOR ATTRACTING
GREAT PUBLICITY

Publicity involves the securing of free 'air space' in any relevant media such as newspapers, magazines, trade journals, public speaking forums and radio or television, for the specific purpose of building company/product name awareness in the marketplace.

Owner–managers of successful small businesses understand that, for them, the most cost-effective and credible way to build and maintain a high level of name awareness is not by advertising or any other form of paid-for promotion, but through the use of publicity.

There are two ways to
secure publicity:
you can report news as
it happens in the normal
course of events, or you
can make it happen by
staging an event.

Send out lots of news releases

Has your company recently won a big export order, achieved record profits or sales figures, hired new staff or built an office extension? Well if any of these kinds of things have just happened in your business, then why not turn it into a publicity opportunity by sending out a news release? If it's news, then there's a good chance it will be printed or get some airtime. You could be getting some excellent coverage in the local or even national news media, and it wouldn't cost you a penny!

When writing a news release there are a few important points to keep in mind. First, it's crucial that you use an eye-catching headline, which makes your story subject matter appear news-like. A good idea is to model it along the lines of the headlines you'd find in the newspapers. Second, readability is all important, so keep it short and sharp and use double spacing with wide margins. For press releases, whenever possible include a photograph, because to the media, a picture really is worth a thousand words! Thirdly, in the main body of the text give the full facts, spelling out the who, what, where, why, how and when of your story—and remember, because you don't have any control over which bits of your story will be used, never give any bad news or say anything negative! Finally, once you've produced your news release, post it out to the news editors of all the relevant media such as TV and radio stations, newspapers, trade journals, hobby and interest magazines and so on.

 ## Try seminar selling

By organising a seminar that provides a genuine service to your industry, you will be creating a high profile publicity event. You'll also be manufacturing an opportunity to sell to a captive audience of dozens of potential customers.

Base the theme of the seminar on a topic that relates to an issue of common and pressing concern in your industry, such as new regulations, competition from abroad or technological change. Make your products and services only a part, albeit an important part, of the seminar. In other words, do a 'covert' not an 'overt' sell. Always put yourself and your company in the role of experts, not salespeople.

Hold the seminar on neutral territory, preferably a plush hotel, and don't forget to invite the press! A good tip is to include other industry experts as speakers if you can—ideally, of course, those who just happen to be your customers, your suppliers or your distributors. That way, while they're talking, they're adding to your company's credibility.

56 Create an award

Through creating a prestigious award bearing your company's name in recognition for a top student at your local university, you'll boost your company's credibility, and create some publicity too. You'll also be forming a valuable alliance with the premier seat of learning in your area. Here is what you do.

Donate an award for the top student taking a degree course in a subject area that's related in some way to your business, and let the professor decide who deserves the award. For example, if you were a clothing manufacturer, then perhaps an award for the top textile design student might well be appropriate. Most importantly, make it a really prestigious-sounding award comprising a cash prize together with a specially designed certificate, framed, signed and dated. Contact the press at the outset, and then at every prize-giving ceremony, so you can maximise its publicity value to the mutual benefit of all parties: your company, the university and the student.

57 Harness local government power

As a champion of local business, your local government representative or Member of Parliament has a vested interest in anything that affects public opinion in a positive way. What's more, they have a highly efficient and influential publicity machine at their disposal. So this idea is all about creating an event of public interest which, albeit indirectly, will engage your local government representative as a willing ambassador for your business.

Firstly, you'll need to create an event that highlights a topical but non-political issue, such as a new export drive or a safety or environmental issue, and one which is linked in some way to the benefits of your product or service. The idea is to provide a ready-made platform for your representative to speak out, for example by opening the event, being a guest speaker or simply being available to answer questions. Anything that guarantees press coverage. Next, be sure to launch the event during a government recess period, when your representative is able to devote time and effort to local issues. Most importantly, however, always put the focus on the issues, and not on your product or service, so that your representative can be seen to remain unbiased. That way, everybody wins. Here is an example of how this idea was used by a car exhaust manufacturer:

A manufacturer of a new type of environmentally friendly car exhaust system was able to attract the local government representative as the key speaker at its official new product launch party. The representative spoke about the need to reduce the harmful effects of exhaust emissions and in so doing, at least indirectly, was seen to endorse the company's product. Needless to say, the speech significantly boosted the publicity surrounding the new product launch and, cheekily, the company was able to maximise its opportunities by promoting the event using the catch-phrase: Vote Xhaustless exhaust systems!

58 Wrestle with a crocodile!

Sometimes doing something silly makes good business sense! In fact, a well managed publicity stunt can be a very effective way of raising your company profile. A publicity stunt is an event or occasion of some kind, which is designed for the specific purpose of attracting the attention of the news media. It can give you blanket exposure across the full range of media, and electrify your image as a company that makes things happen. Here is an example:

The staff of a direct marketing agency once posed naked for a magazine advertisement in order to persuade potential clients that their agency was completely trustworthy! All 25 staff at the company appeared naked in the advertisement. Although legs and arms were carefully positioned to conceal their intimate parts, each member of staff stared squarely into the camera for a photograph that formed the centrepiece of the advertisement. 'We won't be hiding behind the usual protocols' said the ad copy. Within 24 hours of its publication, everyone was talking about it, and not just within media circles. The advertisement captured the imagination of the general public, and national and regional newspapers, TV and radio covered the story. Literally millions of dollars worth of exposure for the price of a full colour one-page advertisement!

When deciding on a publicity stunt, there are a number of factors to bear in mind. For a stunt to attract lots of publicity, it must be inherently interesting, amusing and newsworthy. It must also possess the 'Wow!' factor. Above all, if at all possible, make it in some way appropriate to your product or service. For example, if you run a bakery, perhaps you could stage an attempt to set a new world pie-eating record; or if you are in the travel agency business promoting holidays to the Australian outback, perhaps you should go wrestle with a man-eating crocodile!

59 Conduct a phoney feud

If you operate in a highly competitive local market, a phoney feud is a means by which two competitors can put themselves in the spotlight, and all the rest in the shade, by attracting lots of publicity. A 'phoney feud' takes place when two business rivals hatch a plan to attack each other publicly, generating an escalating war between them by using a series of stage-managed 'tongue in cheek' publicity stunts. It captures the imagination of the public, creates its own publicity momentum, and can turn both rivals into local celebrities.

To make this idea work you must choose your adversary with great care, making sure that both of you are of equal size and status. Most of all, you must be able to trust each other. Devise a plan of attacking each other based purely on fun. For example, disputes around who has the best looking staff, the cleanest delivery vans or most smartly dressed salespeople—that kind of thing. Start the feud with a war of words, and then escalate it into a war of actions, using a series of publicity stunts which, over the space of a few weeks or even months, culminates in a grand showdown between you, and ends the feud in a blaze of publicity.

60 Try the free lunch publicity pact

Sometimes, a little imagination is all it takes to make a big difference to your sales figures, and that's what the 'free lunch' publicity pact is all about. It's a form of contra-deal between a company and one or more of its customers, whereby the company agrees to provide free goods or services in exchange for the opportunity to create some media interest at the customer's expense. Here's a classic example of a how this idea works:

> The owner of a newly built Mexican restaurant found that she'd spent so much money on fixtures and fittings, she didn't have enough money left in the budget to pay for her advertising campaign! In desperation, she went home that night determined to think up some way of promoting her restaurant but without having to spend big dollars. Later on that evening,

when her teenage son returned home sporting a new tattoo symbolising his allegiance to the local football team, the solution to her problem hit her in a flash of inspiration. As a result, some two weeks later, photographers were literally lining up to take pictures of diners in her new restaurant. In addition she was being featured on local radio and TV, and her customers were becoming local celebrities—and all for the price of a $50 classified advertisement! So how did she do it? Well, in the advertisement she simply offered 'free lunches for life' to anyone game enough to have the restaurant's logo—a cactus tree—tattooed on their backside! Of course this was a stunt guaranteed to attract members of her target market (the 18–30s set) as well as plenty of media interest. Apparently, about 50 people responded to the advertisement, with each one agreeing to take part in the restaurant's publicity campaign in exchange for a free lunch whenever they wanted it, and for as long as the restaurant stayed in business.

As you can see, the free lunch publicity pact can be a great way to promote a business. The key is to think up a contra-deal style proposition that is crazy and unusual enough to attract media attention, yet at the same time one that is going to be mutually beneficial to both yourselves and your customers.

61 Use product placements

Ever since Tom Cruise started a craze for Ray-Ban sunglasses in the film *Top Gun*, the deliberate display of branded products within feature films, TV shows and other productions has become big business. It provides mass exposure, and helps products assume a 'movie star' status. Here's how the idea of product placements could be made to work for your company.

Compile a list of the large, multinational, non-competing companies operating in your industry that advertise widely across a variety of media, and with which you would like your products to be associated. Get their names and addresses from advertisements in your trade press. Send a letter addressed to the Marketing Director, offering your products, factories, plant and machinery, office sites, uniforms and vehicles as props and backdrops for inclusion in their advertising and publicity shots. It helps add realism for them and keeps their costs down, while at the same time ensuring that your company gets plenty of free media exposure.

62 Offer your services to the media as an industry expert

This approach can generate lots of media exposure so that as time goes by, in the eyes of the general public, both your name and your company's name will become synonymous with wisdom and respectability, which is just the kind of mega-credibility that money cannot buy.

To become a well known industry expert, simply make yourself available for comment on radio or TV whenever there is a topical issue relating to your industry. Remember, the media are always desperate for an informed comment or quote, so if you make sure you are always ready to give them one, you'll soon be on your way to becoming a media star.

63 Write a one-page article

Magazines and trade publications are continually looking for good articles to publish, and whenever readers read an article of interest to them, the author instantly attracts attention and credibility. This is why it makes a lot of sense to try to get published in any publication that is likely to be read by your prospective customers. (In addition, including a copy of a published article in your company information pack always looks impressive.)

The key factor in getting any editor interested in publishing your article is your choice of topic and its title, which must be of interest to the publication's readers. For example, the owner–manager of a sales training company writing for a business management magazine could write an article entitled:

'Six easy ways for any sales manager to double sales force productivity'

Another example might be the owner–manager of a building company writing for a home and garden magazine. In this case, an article could be submitted entitled:

'The shocking truth about roof and wall insulation,
and how to make sure yours works'

In this way, ensure your article contains some useful ideas that will be helpful to your prospective customers. Also, before submitting your article check its length to ensure it will fit neatly onto one page of your chosen publication. Although there can never be any guarantees that your article will get published, by following these simple guidelines you will be giving yourself the best chance of success.

64 Produce a book

Imagine the prestige value to your company of being associated with an authoritative reference book of immense practical use, and one that is frequently referred to by virtually everyone connected with your industry. Of course, a book like this would be a highly effective promotional tool, enabling both you and your staff to enhance your reputation as leading experts in your field. Well, here's a relatively easy and inexpensive way to achieve all this, together with a blaze of publicity at your book launch.

As you can see from my choice of a title for this idea, I've deliberately put the emphasis on 'producing' a book, not writing one; and with good reason. Clearly, for many owner–managers, writing a book would be much too time consuming; not to mention a hugely daunting task. Hence, the beauty of this idea is that you get *other people* to write the bulk of the book! Although you will need to write one chapter, the remainder of your efforts will be in organising and producing it rather than writing it. Here's how this idea works.

Hand pick about half a dozen or so other professional 'experts' who offer non-competing products and services into your marketplace. For example, if you supply office furniture, then you would need to select people from other businesses connected with the office; for example those who sell computers, photocopiers, telephone equipment, security systems, stationery and so on. Next, invite each one to contribute a chapter towards the book. Explain that the book will be a purchaser's manual and that, as such, each chapter should contain useful 'how to' information and advice for customers, and be written in an informative style (rather than coming across as too much of a hard sell). A good tip is to write your own chapter first, before contacting anyone else, so that you can use it as a means of showing the other contributors what sort of content, format and style is required. Furthermore, be sure to point out the benefits of being involved: not only will each contributor get due recognition as a co-author, but go on to explain that you can guarantee that the book will be circulated to thousands of new prospective customers! This is because each contributor must agree to purchase a minimum number of, say,

500 books (at cost price) to be distributed (free of charge, or sold) to their existing customer base and/or their best 'hot prospect' list. That way, every contributor benefits from the distribution effort of their co-authors, not to mention the pass-along readership that may well double or even triple the original circulation figure. Then coordinate the effort of all your chosen contributors, ensuring they submit their chapter by a certain date.

Most importantly, make sure that the book cover is well designed, and that it prominently features each co-author and the details of their company affiliation. Note that it usually pays to use a professional printing firm to design, print and bind your book. It also makes sense to pitch the recommended retail price for the book as high as you can because it helps strengthen the perception of a high quality/high value book in the eyes of your customers. Finally, don't forget to arrange a glitzy book launch as a means of attracting lots of publicity, to the benefit of everyone involved.

65 Be a good corporate citizen

Here's an example of a good corporate citizen:

> Avon Cosmetics donates a certain percentage of their sales revenue to the Breast Cancer Awareness Institute. This means their sales representatives have an extra benefit to offer to customers. What's more, they can feel especially good about their company, their products and themselves. So while Avon has raised millions of dollars for a worthy cause, sales have continued to go up, and the company has gained plenty of high quality media exposure.

In case you're wondering, this kind of approach doesn't just work for large companies. It can also be used by smaller ones, just like yours. For example, my local dry cleaners periodically supports a school for children with special needs and attracts lots of publicity in the process, both for themselves and for the school. I'm sure that with a little savvy public relations management, you too could associate your firm with a worthy cause, create a higher profile, motivate your staff and pick up some extra customers.

The choice of charity or cause with which to associate your company name is the first and most important decision. Review all the candidate organisations in your local community and choose one that is most likely to attract those people who best fit your target customer profile. In making your approach, spell out all the advantages to both parties and discuss the·

basis upon which you could do business together. This could be in the form of a 'one off' donation (either in cash or by making a gift of your products and services) or, alternatively, some kind of ongoing donation worked out on the basis of a percentage of sales revenue or your operating profits. Always discuss the terms of your arrangements in full detail, including the timeframe involved and the duties and responsibilities of both parties. Ideally, arrange for your company name to be mentioned in their literature and any of their other fundraising activities. Also, ensure you get 'category exclusivity', which means your partner agrees to deal with only one company selling your type of products and services—your company! In addition, make sure they agree to be 'available for comment' on your behalf whenever the need arises as part of your publicity-generating activities.

66 Organise a hole-in-one challenge

If you sell up-scale products, and if it's a well known fact that many people connected with your industry are golf enthusiasts, then this idea could be perfect for attracting the right kind of publicity for your company. It's the simple idea of organising an invitation-only golf tournament for all the VIPs in your industry. However, the exciting twist to this idea is that you offer one of your products (or if this is not feasible, a significant cash prize) to the first player who gets a hole-in-one. Here's an example of how you can make this idea work, but without having to worry that someone might actually win:

Bob, the owner of a sports car dealership, decided to organise a hole-in-one challenge as a means of promoting a new range of sports cars. About 200 previous and current customers were selected from the company's database and invited to a special one-day tournament to be held at one of the top golf clubs in the region. Although a charge was made for each ticket in order that the company could cover the costs of hiring the golf club facilities for the day, the grand prize of a brand new sports car for the first player to score a hole-in-one was strongly promoted as the main attraction. Not only that, but the company also promised to pay a further $50 000 (the value of the car) to a local charity should anyone shoot a hole-in-one.

A few days before the tournament, Bob contacted the press who were only too pleased to provide plenty of media coverage. Photographs of Bob posing with the gleaming new sports car prize and holding up a huge fake cheque appeared in newspapers and on TV, as well as in the golf club newsletter. He couldn't have bought that kind of media exposure! Needless to say, on the day of the tournament, the sports car was proudly on show on the first tee where everyone was keen to have a closer look. What's more, every local news reporter was keen to cover the day's events in the hope that someone would score a hole-in-one. However, much to Bob's dismay—and despite the success of the event and a few dozen very interested new prospective customers—nobody did manage to score a hole-in-one. You see, had somebody actually won then of course the publicity would have been even bigger, and yet it wouldn't have cost Bob another penny, because he'd taken out an insurance policy to cover the risk. Now that's smart marketing!

67 Launch a sticker campaign

Issues such as health, safety, security and the environment demand attention because they are of concern to everyone. This is why a simple, company-branded sticker to warn, deter or remind your customers about one or another of these issues can work well as a publicity tool. When your stickers serve a valuable purpose, it is highly likely that people will want to display them in a place where they are guaranteed to get noticed, which means your company will get noticed too. Here's how one company used the idea of a sticker campaign to their advantage:

An electrical appliance manufacturer launched a 'save electricity' scheme during a time of rising energy costs. People participated in the scheme simply by displaying the company's bright yellow stickers next to light switches and other power sockets in their homes or places of work, as a reminder not to waste electricity. The scheme quickly became so popular it attracted media attention and even gained the backing of a local politician. Against the background of the company logo of a wise owl, the sticker simply read:
Save electricity—switch me off when not in use!
Courtesy of Electro Appliances Ltd

To make a sticker campaign work for you, choose a theme appropriate to both your business and the concerns of your customers and turn it into a campaign. Simple themes tend to work best, such as 'property protected', 'safety first' or 'save energy'. Design an authoritative-looking sticker, in the shape of a triangle or circle. The colour combination should be in keeping with your theme, but make sure it is colourful enough to really stand out. Note that your company name should be featured in a subtle and unobstructive way so that it does not detract from the main message of the campaign. For example, simply use the words 'Supported by' or 'Courtesy of' and then your company name. Your stickers should then be distributed free of charge, as this increases the likelihood that they will get passed around and displayed. A good idea is to distribute them as an insert within a magazine or trade journal aimed at your target customers. With a bit of luck they'll soon attract media attention, but if not, at least they'll be on view all over the place for a very long time to come!

68 Organise a fundraiser

For some free publicity and the opportunity to demonstrate your product and service to a captive audience of dozens of potential customers whilst also helping to raise funds for a worthy cause, organise a fundraiser. Here's an example of what to do and how to do it:

Pam owns and manages The Kitchen Shop, a trendy specialist retail store that sells everything for the kitchen. Upon hearing that a local high school was looking to raise money to build a new gymnasium, Pam contacted them with an idea for how The Kitchen Shop could assist by running an event on the school's behalf—a suggestion which was gratefully and enthusiastically received by the school's fundraising committee. Pam's idea was to offer parents, caregivers, staff and other friends of the school the opportunity to go along to a special evening demonstration showing how to cook quick and healthy family meals by using the latest range of 'infusion' cookware. (At the time, this was a revolutionary new concept in cooking which had just hit the market.) She and her staff would do the demonstrations and then dish up a tasty supper for everyone free of charge as long as the school, for their part, promoted the event, sold the tickets and laid on the venue and cooking facilities. This meant that, while The Kitchen Shop would benefit from a raised company profile and the opportunity to sell their wares to a captive audience, the school would benefit from the revenue on ticket sales.

Needless to say, in the weeks leading up to the event, Pam was delighted to see the school doing a great job in publicising it, not to mention the efforts of a school-wide sales force of highly motivated kids! So much so that on the evening itself, after having sold well over 100 tickets, about 80 people turned up. At $10 per ticket this represented a good return for the school as well as 80 potential new customers for The Kitchen Shop! Certainly a good evening was had by all, and Pam made sure everyone went home with a full stomach and a special discount voucher worth 5 per cent off their next purchase at The Kitchen Shop.

Of course, the beauty of this kind of fundraiser is that it's virtually guaranteed to be successful because those attending can enjoy the 'feelgood' factor associated with doing their bit to help out the local school, scout group, sports club or whatever. In organising a fundraiser, however, be sure to make the event itself as interesting and attractive as possible. By putting the emphasis on entertainment, not business, you'll win more friends and make more sales.

6

IDEAS FOR ADVERTISING
MORE CREATIVELY

Advertising is the use of paid-for space in the mass media, such as in a magazine, a trade journal, a newspaper, or on radio or television, for the purpose of communicating with a company's target customers and persuading them to take some form of action.

Owner–managers of successful small businesses take the view that, when it comes to advertising, trying to out-think their competitors by seeking to be creative and different, is preferable to trying to out-spend them!

The key to successful
advertising is to out-think
your competitors rather
than to out-spend them.

69 Try the information pack prospector

A few years ago when I was the marketing director of a small computer company, I was sifting through the classified advertising column in our local business magazine when the following advertisement caught my eye:

Copy the experts and grow your business fast!
For free information pack, telephone XXXX XXXX, 24 hours.

As you might expect, I telephoned straight away and ordered my free information pack, which turned out to be an interesting pamphlet featuring a series of case studies showing how a national firm of marketing consultants had helped a number of local businesses to dramatically improve their sales. What an excellent promotion, wouldn't you agree? Anyway, it had me thinking—why pay for large, full colour, glossy advertisements if you don't have to? Why not save money and help prospects find you, rather than the other way around, by using the simple and relatively inexpensive method of classified advertising? Even if you don't think it is applicable to your kind of business (and most people don't), why not at least give it a try? You never know, it might actually work, and if it does, you could be dramatically cutting your average cost of sale.

When placing an information pack prospector, choose the most appropriate classified section of a newspaper, business magazine or trade journal. It is best to keep the content of your ad short and sharp, advertising the benefits of your offer, rather than the product or service itself. Request that they call your 24-hour answering machine to obtain their free information pack. The information pack should be of genuine value to your prospects, but should work for you in moving the customer towards a purchase decision. Common examples include the insurance company's guide to the finance maze, the catering company's wedding arrangement checklist or the consulting company's top ten profit-boosting ideas.

70 Activate your print advertising

On a limited budget there is only one type of successful print advertising: *direct response advertising*. This means that your magazine or newspaper advertisements must include a 'call to action' requesting readers to place an order, arrange a sales visit or send for further information. The main advertising activators are:

1 Ring us now!

2 Return this coupon! (by mail or fax)

3 Call in and see us! (and bring this voucher with you)

4 Email us now!

Without a call to action, not only is your advertising failing to sell but, worse still, its success rate is not measurable. If you can't count the responses you get, then every time you place a repeat advertisement how do you know you're not just throwing good money after bad? For these reasons, I am convinced that any other form of print advertising is quite simply a luxury most small businesses can't afford.

Whenever you've placed a direct response advertisement, always take the time to evaluate its effectiveness in terms of the number and types of responses obtained, your costs per response, inquiry-to-sale conversion rates and so on. Most importantly, be sure to document this information so that, as time goes by, you can compare one style of advertising with another, and one type of publication with another, to see what works best.

71 Run a word-game poster campaign

If you want to develop a greater awareness of your business among the general public in your local area, make a note of the following example:

A new garden centre had just opened on the outskirts of a large town. The owners wanted to make the general public aware of it and its location. To this end, the following poster was displayed on a number of billboards around town:

NEED GARDEN STUFF?

Come ot su, ew evah ti lla !

Gardenworld 🌲
(opposite Zoo)

Did you find yourself re-reading the poster in order to work out what it says? Well if so, then you've already discovered the power of this idea in attracting people's attention and engaging their thought processes! I hope you'll agree that it's easy to see why some form of word-game gimmick like this works so well in a poster advertising campaign. Most people are naturally curious and simply can't resist the challenge of deciphering the words and of course, when they do, they're far more likely to remember the sales message.

When devising an appropriate word game for your poster campaign, there are a couple of key factors to bear in mind. First, only ever use odd spelling or an unusual word layout as the basis for your game because these approaches are highly visual and work well in drawing people's attention to your poster. Above all, however, pay close attention to the level of difficulty of your word game. Test it out on your family and friends. If you find that most of them have to think for a few moments before experiencing a mild sense of satisfaction at having cracked your code, then you can be sure you've got it about right. Second, make sure your word game doesn't dominate the poster to the exclusion of all other information. Always take the opportunity to communicate your company name, location and contact details with absolute clarity.

72 Make every 25th customer a winner!

Here's an example of this idea:

> My local car tyre and exhaust centre runs this promotion every year for about four weeks during a period when business is a little slack. The company owner is featured in a series of short radio and newspaper advertisements, explaining that every 25th customer who buys new tyres or an exhaust system from him gets their purchase absolutely free. It's a winning formula for two reasons. First, it's such a simple idea that everyone can understand exactly how the promotion works. Second, people are always attracted by the idea of winning something without having to risk anything. After all, who could resist the chance of saving themselves the price of a new set of tyres, just for the sake of going to one garage rather than another?

This promotion can easily be adapted and made to work for a wide range of different businesses. The first thing is to do your sums. Base your calculations on the amount of profit you make from the average sale, the costs of promoting your offer, and your estimation of the additional sales you'll generate. Then work out the frequency with which you can comfortably afford to give a customer their money back while still making an overall profit. For example, the owner of the car tyre centre had worked out that he could afford to make one customer a winner out of every 25; but for you, this could work out to be one out of every 10, 20 or maybe 30 customers.

Next, you have to decide how you're going to administer your offer. In other words, how are your customers going to know if they're the 10th, 20th or 25th customer? If you use numbered invoices, then one way would be to simply stamp every 25th invoice with the word 'Congratulations!' in advance of the promotion. Alternatively, you could arm your counter staff or salespeople with a roll of raffle tickets, and just after each customer pays they are given the next ticket so they can see if it's divisible by 25 (or whatever your winning frequency happens to be).

Promote your offer vigorously in all the relevant media, making sure to explain how the promotion works and stating the time period over which it will be run. Also note that, because there's an important trust factor involved with this kind of promotion, it's always a good idea to feature yourself in the advertising if you can. People are always reassured when they can see that the owner–manager of the business is prepared to put their own reputation on the line.

73 Do a deadline deal

If you advertise regularly in a particular publication, then here is a way to negotiate additional space, but at a rock bottom price. It's called a 'deadline deal' because every publisher has a copy deadline, and as that deadline draws near, so too does the threat of unsold, leftover ad space. So an arrangement whereby your publisher can fill any leftover spaces with your usual advertising copy, but at a pre-arranged ultra-low price, creates a win–win result for both of you.

When negotiating a deadline deal, remember that because you're already a regular advertiser, you've got some real negotiating power. So strike a hard bargain, and don't agree to pay more than a fraction of the usual prices. Simply agree to have your ad squeezed into any space anywhere in the publication, but without the need for them to seek your prior approval. That way, all you'll receive is a smaller invoice and bigger exposure!

74 Share your advertising with customers

If you sell to businesses, imagine this: a full page, full colour, glossy advertisement that costs you about half the price it should have done, and one that features several of your best customers all saying great things about your business! Well this is what shared advertising is all about. It's when you lay off a substantial part of the costs by giving your customers a chance to advertise themselves under your umbrella for a modest fee, so long as they say something nice about you.

Choose a publication that you know is widely read by people in your marketplace, and ask the advertising representative to quote you their standard rates for placing full colour advertisements in a range of different sizes, from a full page all the way down to the smallest box. The next task is to design your advertisement. There are a number of different layouts you could use (look out for examples in your trade press), but the most basic is simply to run your usual copy right in the centre of the page, and then surround it with a number of smaller display boxes for advertising your customers' businesses. Next, send your best customers a mock-up of your intended advertisement and invite them to advertise in one of the display boxes. The advantage of buying a full page is that the price of the smaller boxes works out much cheaper than the normal rate, so you can pass these savings on to your customers. In return, make it clear that all they have to do is give you a good quote, and/or simply identify themselves as one of your many satisfied customers.

75 Record tele-message ads

When an inquirer has telephoned and is put on hold (while their call is being transferred or redirected), or when you are not available and they are listening to your answering message, it's one of those few occasions when you've got 100 per cent of their attention. So be sure to make the most of this opportunity by providing callers with a useful pre-recorded sales information service. For small businesses, a short promotional message personally delivered by the owner–manager always works well. It's a simple and effective way of advertising, and at no extra cost to the business. In short, it's a no-brainer. Go to it!

76 Make the most of directory advertisements

The Yellow Pages and other similar telephone directories are still the first place most prospective customers will go to find the names, addresses and telephone numbers of potential suppliers. Most importantly, searching a directory usually means they are already in a buying frame of mind. This is why a directory advertisement is arguably one of the most important pieces of advertising that you will ever do.

Ideally, your advertisement should be immediately noticeable and stand out from those of your competitors listed on the same page. This can be achieved by using a large bold typeface, a simple layout, a strong border and a line drawing or photograph. When deciding on what to say, the main thing is to tell customers what they want to hear, and no more. Anything else is pure clutter. Usually, this necessitates that you use a big heading emphasising your main customer benefit and explaining why they should come to you. The key to deciding on your heading is to put yourself in the prospective customer's shoes and imagine what is likely to be going through their mind as they search for a telephone number. A good example of this is a headline for 'Pete the Plumber':

> If you want a plumber who always turns up on time,
> doesn't leave a mess,
> and never charges above the quotation—call Pete.

This headline tells prospective customers exactly what they want to hear and has the added advantage of a little humour. Notably, the biggest mistake you can make is to feature your company name as the headline. This is because a prospect is usually searching for a solution and not your company's name! After the headline, the only other essential ingredients would normally be your company name, address, email address and of course your telephone number, which should always be featured prominently.

77 Try the second-hand prospector method

Here's a way of unlocking a whole new market for your product and one that is already out there, ready and waiting! A 'shadow market' occurs whenever there is a healthy second-hand market, as there often is with products such as computers or power tools—in fact almost anything, from sewing machines to combine harvesters. With this method you attract those customers who would otherwise consider themselves as second-hand buyers only, but who just don't fully appreciate the benefits of buying new. Here is what to do.

Place a short classified ad in the 'second-hand items for sale' section of the local newspaper or your trade press and advertise one of your products at a bargain price. Make sure that it is a genuine second-hand offer, such as an ex-demonstration model or a product you've been using in the office. Invite replies to be left on your 24-hour answering machine.

On the message, identify yourself, explaining that you will sell the second-hand product to the first caller who leaves their name and number. However, go on to explain that if any caller is interested in finding out more about a special 'once in a lifetime' offer on a new one, all they have to do is to say so on their message. Within a few days you will have generated a tidy number of hot prospects drawn directly from the shadow market—prospects who you wouldn't ordinarily have been able to reach. Then, after you've sold your bargain product to the first inquirer, contact all the others. Apologise to them about the fact that you've already sold the advertised product to the first inquirer, but take the opportunity to spell out the benefits of buying new, because with your warranty and finance terms it will seem hardly worth their while buying second-hand!

78 Offer a front-end trade-in

If you operate in a market where there's a lot of price competition, there's always a great temptation to join in the scramble to offer the largest possible discounts just to try and get your share of the business. However, instead of offering a discount, you could offer a 'front-end trade-in'. This enables you to differentiate yourself by offering customers a generous trade-in value on their old one when they buy a new one from you. For example, a double-glazing company could invite people to trade in their old window frames for new sealed units. The fascinating thing about this idea is that, the more obsolete or worthless customers see their old item as being, the more compelling your offer becomes. In addition, the more unusual it is to offer a trade-in deal in your type of market, the more seductive its effect in attracting new customers. Here are some other key points to remember. First, set the trade-in value as high as possible so your offer sounds almost too good to be true, but remember never to set it at a cost which exceeds the normal discount you would have given away anyway! Second, if replacement is very inconvenient for the customer— as it so often is with large, heavy or dirty items such as lawnmowers or furniture—then why not offer to take it away as part of the deal. As you'll appreciate, offering a service like this can make a huge difference to the effectiveness of this kind of promotion.

79 Offer a back-end trade-in

In contrast to a front-end trade-in—a promotion designed to pull in first time customers with a trade-in that takes place at the point of purchase— a back-end trade-in is designed to go one step further by guaranteeing the customer a generous trade-in value when they come to replace the product they're buying from you now. In other words, the actual trade-in takes place at the back end of the sale (as it were) rather than the front end; thereby acting as an incentive for the customer to buy another one from you, and not from the competition. Hence, it's a promotion that only applies to those products with inherent depreciation and which customers know they are going to have to replace sooner or later, such as a car. As you can see, this kind of promotion is a great way to effectively lock out the competition, because you're simultaneously offering customers a reason to buy from you now and a reason to come back to buy from you again later. In offering a back-end trade-in, here are the key points to remember.

In your advertising, explain that the reason why you can guarantee such a generous trade-in value is because your product is of such high quality. Clearly state that the offer has no effect on the initial purchase price: trade-in or no trade-in the price is the same. Most importantly, present customers with a written guarantee as a reminder that they should come back and buy from you. Finally, always get back in contact with purchasers when you know the product is likely to be nearing the end of its lifespan. That way, neither of you will miss out on the opportunity to cash in on this offer.

80 Make yours a prized product

Why not link up with a publication serving your market and launch a competition that gives readers a chance to win your product as the star prize? It's a great way to generate a widespread interest in your product. Here is what to do.

The first step is to choose a host publication aimed at your target customers and one with the kind of image with which you'd like to be associated. Next, you'll need to think through the details of exactly how the competition is going to work, making sure its theme is in keeping with the nature of your product. For example, if your business is a travel company then a competition in which the first person to correctly answer five questions about an exotic South Sea island wins a trip there, would be appropriate. Most importantly, build into the competition as many advantages as possible to the host publication so that you can persuade them that it's going to be worth their while getting involved. To continue our example, your travel company could promise to provide all competition entrants with a free travel guide, or something else that's going to be attractive to their readers.

81 Try cinema advertising

Most small business owner–managers rarely give cinema advertising a second thought. Either they believe it's an old fashioned medium that's had its day, or that it only works for the large multi-national companies, or that it's too expensive. Well, perhaps there is more than a grain of truth in all of these observations, but not for all small companies. The fact is, cinema is currently experiencing a new surge in popularity around the world and, under the right circumstances, the big screen can be an extremely effective advertising medium for a local small business. Here's an example:

> A gourmet burger restaurant aimed at 18–35 year olds was located only 200 metres from a cinema complex in the centre of town. Since it was apparent that many of the films being shown in the early evenings were attracting large audiences of younger adults, the restaurant owner decided to advertise to selected cinema audiences as part of the pre-film programming that screens just before the feature film begins. His advertisement was cheap to produce and cleverly designed so as not to compete with the other glossy, more sophisticated advertisements being shown in the same time slot. Starting with a blank, black screen, lines of white text appeared line by line, with the only audio track being a voiceover of the owner reading the text out loud as it came up on screen:
> We hope you enjoy the film.
> When it's over, here's what to do:
> When you exit the film theatre,
> turn right and walk 200 metres down the street.
> (At this point a map appears briefly on screen.)
> When you see the Gourmet Burger Experience Restaurant, stop walking, go in and order one of our delicious burgers.
> Hand over your cinema ticket, and we'll even give you a free portion of fries to go with your burger.
> Go on, treat yourself to the new Gourmet Burger Experience.
> (At this point a picture of a gourmet burger appears on screen.)
> They're delicious!
> See you soon …

As this example clearly illustrates, the beauty of cinema advertising is that you have a large captive audience, the ability to measure response rates (via the movie tickets promotion), and plenty of scope for targeting your market by different types of films/audiences as well as by the time of day, day of the week and so on. What's more, with a little creativity and imagination, your film need not cost much to produce and doesn't have to compete with the big budget productions in order to be effective.

82 Make the most of your signage

The first rule of advertising is that you must get noticed, which is why it's important to make the most of your signage. To put it another way, while you're busily working away on the inside of your business, your signage should be busily working away on the outside! In fact, your company's premises and its geographic location are ready made marketing assets that you can use to seize the attention of passers-by and potential customers with one or more of the following attention-grabbing techniques:

- *Promotion-based grabbers* attract people's attention by making them an offer, such as a roadside cafe that advertises a free coffee to all drivers. An excellent way to communicate your offer is to erect a huge blackboard. Not only is a blackboard an attention grabber in its own right, but it also makes it easy for you to change your offer on a regular basis. For example, I often drive past a finance company that uses a blackboard and whitewash paint to promote their special offer of the month, which at the moment reads like this:

  How does your retirement plan stack up?
  FREE analysis this month!
  Tel: XXXX XXXX

- *Product-based grabbers* exploit the fun factor and make your company instantly recognisable. For maximum effectiveness, however, they must be relevant to your product. For example, the car crashed half way through the wall of the body repair shop, or the inflatable super rat sitting on the roof of the pest control company—or how about an optical illusion painted across the entire outside facia of a graphic design company. Of course, another advantage of product-based attention grabbers like these is their potential for generating plenty of publicity spin-off in the local media.

Location-based grabbers exploit where you say it rather than how you say it. For example, if you're located below a flyover, paint your message on the roof; or if you back on to a railway or a major roadway, put your message at the rear. Better still if, like the last pub in Scotland, your location is a landmark of some description, use your signage to tell the world about it!

83 Blow them away with a blow-out sale

A blow-out sale is exactly what it says. It's the simple idea of organising a high profile, one-day only, cut price sale on a selected number of product lines as a way of getting people in through the door and moving some stock. It's a great way to create a swirl of marketplace awareness, and to attract plenty of new and existing customers. Although normally associated with retail stores, a blow-out sale can work just as well for many other types of businesses too. From a pizza parlour offering unbelievable 'meals deals', to a camping equipment manufacturer wanting to clear out old stocks, it's a tried and tested formula that can serve a valuable purpose for many companies.

When organising your blow-out sale, the most important ingredient is that you create a good reason for having it in the first place. For example, it could be part of a grand opening or re-opening extravaganza, a company birthday celebration or a customer appreciation (thank you) day. You will also need to decide on a 'loss leader' item. This is one of your most popular products that you can sell for a ridiculously low price and that is guaranteed to act as a drawcard, so that you can use it to spearhead your advertising and promotional campaign. Although you should be prepared to make a substantial 'loss' on your loss leader, it's also a 'leader' because it pulls in the customers and leads to plenty of additional business on other items in your sale. In fact, the principle of the loss leader is that the more you're prepared to lose, the greater its magnetic effects and the more other business you're likely to win!

Advertise and promote your blow-out sale vigorously in all the relevant media, about four to seven days beforehand. Make sure to highlight your 'loss leader' deal, explain the reason for the sale and emphasise the fact that it's for one day only and at one location only. If appropriate, write to your top customers and invite them individually. One last point. It's always worth considering issuing 'bounce back' certificates to all purchasers at your blow-out sale. A bounce back certificate is a special discount voucher redeemable against the customer's next purchase and may relate to one or more selected items. Providing your offer is time fused, bounce back certificates can have the effect of generating a healthy flow-on of extra sales from your newly created client bank.

84 Try the cartoon-style newspaper ad

If you're like most people, then whenever you're flicking through the local newspaper, one of the few items that will almost always catch your eye is the daily cartoon. It normally appears in the same place on about the second or third page, and typically provides a brief, light hearted and often satirical commentary on the news of the day. The point is, people are drawn to it because they've conditioned themselves to look out for the daily cartoon and this is the very reason why this style of newspaper ad can work so well. Here's an example:

A commercial real estate company used the cartoon-style advertisement to boost its listings. The company's initial task was to identify an appropriate theme for attracting the attention of businesspeople who had commercial properties to sell. As always, the best themes are those which relate directly to the needs and wants of a selected target audience. Therefore, in this case it was decided that for busy businesspeople trying to sell commercial real estate, the key theme should be stress reduction. The next step was to imagine a number of stressful situations with which members of the company's target audience would easily be able to identify themselves. A shortlist of six was then chosen to be used in the advertising campaign. For example, one idea was of a stressed-out businessman trapped behind a desk piled high with paperwork and with little spare time to devote to anything else. Another idea was of a buyer running away from a vendor who was desperately pulling on the buyer's shirt, trying to prevent him from leaving without at least making an offer! A local artist was then commissioned to draw the cartoons in a similar style to the one in the local newspaper so that, at first glance, a reader might easily mistake the company's cartoons for the newpaper's regular feature cartoon. When booking the advertising space the company also specified that it wanted to place its six cartoon-style advertisements on the weekly business page of the newspaper (one per week for six weeks), making sure that the ad would appear on the same part of the page every week. This meant its ads would reach business readers who, with a bit of luck, would acquire the habit of looking out for them.

To give you an idea of what the real estate company's cartoons looked like, imagine a 9 × 11 centimetre rectangle with a black border. In the top left hand corner was always a small company name badge, with 90 per cent of the remaining space featuring the cartoon. In the bottom right hand corner, however, the message read:

> For our free, eight-page guide to
> stress free real estate marketing
> telephone us now on XXXX XXXX (24 hrs)

85 Place advertorials in large companies' newsletters

Have you ever considered the advantages of advertising in large companies' newsletters? Think about it. Most small businesses operate in an industry dominated by at least one or two major nationwide or multi-national corporates—large companies that offer a wide range of non-competing products and services into the same marketplace. In fact, just the kind of companies that typically produce top quality, highly respected customer newsletters and post them out directly to a massive audience of active purchasers on a regular basis! The point I'm trying to make is that, in many ways, large companies' newsletters are one of the best advertising mediums around—not only because they are so well targeted, but also because smaller firms are able to benefit from the 'halo effect' of being seen to be associated with the big name players. Best of all, however, are the relatively minimal costs involved (if any), due to the fact that newsletter editors are often stuck for interesting new material and will welcome your submission with open arms.

When seeking to advertise in large companies' newsletters, your first task is to identify the best ones to approach. Start off by compiling a list of all those newsletters which are currently being sent out to customers in and around your marketplace—your customers will help you track them down. Then select the best one from the list, ensuring that the company producing the newsletter is serving the same market as you are, but with complementary (and non-competing) products and services. Next, put together an 'advertorial' for inclusion in your selected newsletter. An advertorial is a cross between an advertisement and an editorial-style write-up. It's an ideal format for newsletters because, providing it serves the purpose of being of genuine interest to readers, most editors will be prepared to turn a blind eye to the fact that it also doubles as a thinly disguised advertisement for your business. When writing the advertorial, put the emphasis on educating readers about a particularly interesting or unusual aspect of your product or service, so that you are adopting an indirect rather than direct selling approach, and don't forget to include your contact details. In addition, copy the typestyle, layout and format of the newsletter itself so that when you submit your advertorial to the editor, you'll be maximising your chances of getting it published 'as is'.

86 Advertise a free information booklet

FREE!!! It's a well known fact that this word is one of the most powerful in advertising, which is why advertising a free information booklet is a great way to generate sales leads. Here's an example of this idea in action.

'Ergonomix' is a small company that specialises in making customised, high quality, ergonomically designed office furniture. After an initial period of great success, the company suddenly found itself with a half-empty order book. Desperate to book appointments with some new prospective customers, the company's salesperson realised she had finally exhausted her own list of contacts and would have to find a new source of sales leads—but from where? Fortunately, the solution soon became apparent when she tried advertising a free information booklet in a nationwide business magazine. The advertisement was immediately successful in generating a flood of hot prospects that she was then able to follow up later with a telephone call. The headline read:

Suffering from Office *STRESS?*
When it comes to reducing stress in the office, we wrote the book.
Now it's yours. FREE...

Beneath the headline was a large photograph of their free information booklet entitled 'Twenty Tips for Reducing Stress in the Office', together with a small piece of copy outlining the benefits of using Ergonomix office furniture as part of a well designed total office environment. Finally, the last part of the ad included a call to action, encouraging readers to pick up the phone to order their free copy of the booklet.

Obviously, the key to this idea is to offer a booklet that is going to be of genuine interest to your target customers, as well as one which is closely associated with your company's product or service, so as to help 'prime the sale' before you make your follow-up telephone call. Above all, it's important to come up with a great title. It's also worth noting that your booklet doesn't need to be more than 8–12 pages long, and that it certainly doesn't (necessarily) need to be elaborately or expensively produced.

87 Consider the two-part radio ad

If you sell direct to the general public and there's a local radio program serving an audience profile that matches your target market, then you should consider the 'two-part radio ad'. It's a powerful formula that persuades listeners to pick up the telephone and place an order.

This idea is called the 'two-part' radio ad because it is pre-recorded in two separate parts. The first part comprises a series of two or three brief testimonials from your existing satisfied customers. Let's say your product is a natural healthcare remedy that helps ease the pain of stiff joints for the over 60s. Then in this case, the first part of your ad would simply feature your best customers saying how bad they felt before taking the remedy compared with how good they felt after having used it. This kind of personal recommendation is a highly credible way of illustrating the benefits of your product, and enables other listeners with a similar problem to 'self-identify' as being members of your target market. Most importantly, however, make sure that at the end of this part of the ad you feature yourself (in your capacity as the owner–manager of the business), giving details of your special offer and the toll-free telephone number to ring. It's very important to add the personal touch to this style of advertisement.

The second part of the two-part radio ad is when the radio program host apparently interviews you on the telephone about your new wonder product. In actual fact, this part of your ad is highly scripted and is pre-recorded in a studio, using sound effects to recreate the feeling of a live telephone interview. Of course, the key to a good script is for the interviewer to ask all the kinds of questions that would be likely to be running through the minds of potential customers; in other words, asking questions on behalf of the listener. The last part of the interview should then be scripted in such a way that you are able to enthusiastically promote your special offer, telling people to place their order now by ringing your toll-free telephone number.

When booking the air space, be sure to target the best possible audience at the best possible time of day. To continue our example, for a healthcare product aimed at the over 60s, this might well be a local radio station's afternoon show. Needless to say, the beauty of the two-part radio ad is that, depending on the time slots and 'package deals' available to advertisers, it can work just as well as one large ad, or as two separate smaller 'stand alone' ads. The point is, to be successful, a special offer advertised on radio needs to be repeated as often as possible, and in this respect the two-part radio ad has built-in flexibility based on the fact that each part reinforces the other.

88 Feature yourselves in a feature page ad

If your business involves an element of project management or the overseeing of some kind of collaborative effort with fellow suppliers, then this idea can be a relatively inexpensive yet highly effective way of showcasing your work and generating new inquiries. A 'feature page' advertisement is when you and your business partners share the cost of a full page spread (including a mix of an editorial-style article and advertisements) relating to a project you've recently completed. Here's an example:

> A house builder wanted to stimulate new inquiries from people thinking of building a new home. To this end, he placed a 'feature page' advertisement in the house and garden section of the local newspaper. In the top left hand third of the page was an editorial-style article about a house his company had just finished building. Under the headline 'Latest McElwain Home Now Available for Public Viewing', the article was accompanied by a photograph of the house, and detailed its various features—the choice of colour schemes used, its design and layout and so on. Notably, the article also highlighted the names of all the local companies that had been used as subcontractors or suppliers, as well as the brand names of all the various building materials used. The remainder of the page was divided up into smaller boxes which were then offered as advertising spaces to each of his fellow suppliers: plumbers, roofing contractors, gasfitters, electricians, plasterers, painters and decorators, window and door manufacturers, etc. Most importantly, however, the builder reserved the space in the bottom right hand corner of the page for his own advertisement. The headline for this advertisement read:
>
> Thinking of Building?
> Call McElwain Builders now on xxxx xxxx for a prompt,
> obligation free quote.

As you can see, the feature page approach is a great way to provide an impressive 'shop window' for both your business and those of your fellow suppliers. It's an informative and interesting read that puts your business in the spotlight, but at a fraction of the cost of a normal full page advertisement.

89 Advertise on other companies' web sites

If your product or service lends itself to being advertised through another company's web site, and you can afford to pay them a reasonable commission on any sales made, then you should seriously consider this idea. Otherwise referred to as online 'affiliate advertising', it's a way of increasing your promotional reach but at no extra cost. This is because, unlike most other forms of advertising, you don't pay for the advertising itself—you only pay a commission as and when it results in a sale. Here's the story of how this idea came about:

Amazon.com, the world's first online bookseller, is reputed to have also been the first company to introduce an online affiliate advertising program. Apparently, the idea came about when Jeff Bezos, Amazon's founder, was chatting with a friend who happened to comment that she would like to sell books off her web site on the subject of coping with divorce, as this would provide an extra service to her web site visitors whilst at the same time generating an extra source of revenue. Jeff immediately realised the massive marketing potential of this idea. If other companies were to advertise selected books which matched the interests of their target customers, then Amazon.com would quickly gain access to a wide range of different market segments, and in a way which would be of mutual benefit to all parties. From a technical point of view, all that would be required was a direct and traceable link that took potential book purchasers straight from each of his affiliates' web sites through to Amazon.com. Hence, the concept of online affiliate advertising was born and the rest, as they say, is history.

In setting up an online affiliate advertising program for your business, make a note of the following steps. First, you'll need to create a shortlist of candidate firms whose customers are likely to be interested in purchasing your products and services, and who already have a professional-looking web site. Secondly, you'll need to talk to an Internet expert about the technical aspects of running your intended program. There are a variety of ways to set up such a program (and different ways to compensate your affiliate) and you will need to discuss the pros and cons of each and decide on the best one for your business. Thirdly, you'll need to telephone each potential affiliate and put forward your proposition. Clearly explain the benefits to them, including your commission structure, and offer to send a written proposal for their consideration. Above all, always sell your company and its products and services as being the kind with which they would be proud to be associated.

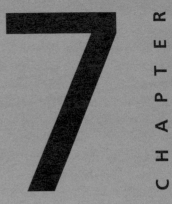

7

IDEAS FOR USING DIRECT MAIL MORE EFFECTIVELY

Direct mail involves the mailing of some form of promotional material direct to selected existing customers and/or prospective new customers, for the purpose of securing repeat business or generating new sales leads.

Owner–managers of successful small businesses understand the importance of personalised, one-to-one communication. Consequently, they direct a constant flow of highly targeted offers to selected groups of both existing and prospective new customers.

Effective direct mail
addresses the largest
possible audience, one
at a time.

90 Conduct testing trials

If you sell products that are re-purchased on a regular basis, this is a way for you to re-establish contact with lapsed customers who, for whatever reason, have stopped buying from you. When you're updating or making improvements to your existing product range, this idea involves getting back in contact and offering a free sample (or free product trial) in return for their cooperation in providing you with some marketing information. Not only will you be getting the essential marketing feedback you need, but with a bit of luck, you will also be taking the first step in turning those old buyers and into new-found customers.

The first thing to do is to dig out your lapsed customer files and compile a 'hit list' of suitable names and telephone numbers. Then telephone each one and request their permission to take part in your testing trials, which simply means testing out your new product ideas and modifications. Clearly explain that they would receive a free sample and that all they have to do is answer a few simple questions. Next, post them the sample together with a covering letter, a simple feedback questionnaire, and a 'test market fact sheet' detailing the product improvements you have made. Note that you should not include any sales information. However, do provide an incentive for them to fax back your questionnaire by a certain date in the form of a special 'thank you' discount voucher, redeemable against any future purchases they may wish to make.

91 Run a questionnaire campaign

Here's the story of one of the most successful direct mailing campaigns I ever came across:

> The sales staff of a small company that specialised in providing sophisticated computerised telephone systems to large organisations were experiencing great difficulty in booking appointments with a number of potential buyers. To address this problem a mailing piece was built around the simple idea of providing an incentive (a department store gift voucher) for these buyers to complete and return a questionnaire which enabled the company to assess the needs of each of these difficult prospects. Needless to say, once a questionnaire had been returned, booking an appointment to go and see each prospect was made much easier because the salesperson was able to promise a specific proposal as to how their current telephone system could be improved.

If your company has a similar problem, then with a little adaptation I'm sure this approach could be made to work equally well. Here's how to go about it. The first step is to compile a list of mailing targets, making sure you have the full name of the person to whom you should send the questionnaire. Next, design a one-page questionnaire that will enable you to make an assessment of each prospect's needs for your product or service. Most importantly, keep the questionnaire very short and easy to fill out. Enclose an explanatory covering letter together with an incentive to participate in the form of a free voucher redeemable at a department store or somewhere similar. The value of the vouchers needn't be much, but it has the effect of obligating respondents to take part.

92   Try the three-dimensional exhibition close

At your next trade exhibition, the 'three-dimensional exhibition close' enables you to attract exactly the type of customers with whom you want to do business. It also guarantees that they will visit your stand and that they'll want to receive a follow-up sales visit. What's more, with this idea, there's no need to spend a small fortune trying to outshine your competitors with a bigger and better exhibition stand.

Here's how to do it. About two weeks before the exhibition, mail out a personalised letter to all the top prospects on your current hit list—the ones you'd really like to see. In your letter, invite them to visit your stand at the exhibition and enclose an unusual and mysterious gift that relates in some way to your business. For example, if you were from a plastic moulding company you could send them a small plastic funnel. In referring to your gift, tell them it would be well worth their time to visit your stand in order to find out more.

At the exhibition, when your invited customers visit your stand, introduce yourself, thank them for coming, and then present them with the second component part of your gift. Make sure it's something they are likely to value. To continue our example, as a follow-up to the plastic funnel you could give them a full colour guidebook to home brewing or wine making.

Immediately after the exhibition is over, telephone to arrange an appointment to deliver the final essential ingredient of their gift. To follow through our example, this could be a complete beer making or wine making kit. This completes the jigsaw and means that what would otherwise have been a difficult appointment to make is now made much easier. Obviously you'll need to think through the best kind of gift to use in your business—one that would appeal to customers, break down into three components and be cost-effective. However, with a little adaptation, it's an approach which can work extremely well for any small business looking for an effective way to compete with larger competitors at their next trade show.

93 Try doing a post office box-out

If you're like most people, you're probably fairly sceptical about the idea of post office box-outs—that's when you arrange with the post office for a piece of mail to be distributed to every box-holder's pigeon hole within a specified location. I used to feel exactly the same way until I was hired by a firm of management consultants to boost their sales. Surprisingly, one of the most successful ideas we came up with was a novel approach to doing a post office box-out. Here's how we did it.

Keep the format of your flyer simple. Don't worry about using any gimmicks. All you need for this idea is one side of a single sheet of A4 or A5 paper, and high quality print. Design the flyer so that the bottom third of the sheet is in the form of a return coupon so that prospects can send off for your free no-obligation information pack. Collect a few examples of different styles of return coupon that other companies have used and model yours on the one you like best. Now, here comes the clever part. In the top two-thirds of the sheet (the space above the coupon), feature a large head-and-shoulders photograph of an existing customer who is a well known businessperson in the local area, together with a quote expressing how they have benefited from using your product or service. To make the text really stand out, use quotation marks and highlight the name of the businessperson and their company.

The quote is a powerful way to hammer home the benefits of your product or service, but it's the photo that really pulls in the inquiries because it adds the kind of 'next door neighbour' credibility that appeals to local box holders. Of course, this means that to make the most of this idea, you'll need to feature a local customer for each mailing centre. However, you'll find most people are only too willing to help because they just can't resist the opportunity to get plenty of free exposure for themselves and their business.

Launch a midnight fax attack!

The 'fax flyer' guarantees your offer will receive urgent attention and won't be forced to compete with your competitors' offers in the morning mail tray. It's quick, it's cheap (due to low night rates) and it has added impact because it's different. Here's what to do.

Every evening before you leave the office, program your fax machine to transmit a personalised sales offer to a selected customer or prospect, timed to go out at midnight. Make your message 'mirror the medium' by including some form of urgency incentive. For example, you might say:

> A response before 10 o'clock in the morning qualifies you for a special introductory discount.

Invite a reply by telephone only in order to initiate a personal dialogue between you and your customer. Mark the front sheet for urgent attention and ensure that the second sheet clearly states your entire offer at a single glance.

An alternative approach is simply to fax a copy of your latest print advertisement or classified advert (ringed with a pencil), and write in the corner something like this:

> Thought you might be interested in this.
> Regards, Geoff

Incidentally, it is worth noting that you should be cautious about using fax flyers as a method of unsolicited advertising because, unlike other methods, the recipient has to pay for the paper to receive your fax message. This means that if you send them out indiscriminately, you're likely to irritate some recipients. So the best way to avoid upsetting people is to telephone beforehand to ask if they would like to receive, by fax, any special offers you might have. You could even remind them of this on your flyer, so that it is seen in a positive light as a special 'fax promotion' service you are offering them. If necessary, you could also tell them that you deliberately timed it to go out at midnight to ensure it did not tie up their fax line during business hours. Finally, the golden rule of sending fax flyers is to only use them for business-to-business advertising. It's an invasion of privacy to send them to people at home, and especially in the middle of the night when it could awaken the whole household!

95 Do a boomerang video shot

If you've ever wondered how you could justify the extra cost of using videos as a method of promotion, check out the following example:

> An independent supermarket operator used this idea when he opened a new store. He had videotapes delivered to all the households in his catchment area showing people the benefits of shopping at his new superstore, but cleverly offered to exchange the video for an in-store voucher that customers could redeem against their first basket of shopping. This incentive not only ensured that tapes were returned and could be used again, but successfully achieved his objective of getting potential customers to change their shopping habits and try out his new store.

If you think this idea might be applicable to your business, then here's how to go about putting it to work. Keep the video short and straight to the point. It should first focus on the key benefits of your product and service and then tempt customers to bring the video with them into your store or place of business. Clearly explain exactly how the tape-for-discount exchange deal will work. Keep the format simple. In fact, it could even be a simple head-and-shoulders shot of you delivering a personal message to the camera—perhaps interspersed with a few stills. You don't need a Hollywood-sized budget to put your business in the picture! Having said that, it always makes sense to try out this idea on a small scale at first, just to see if it is going to work out to be cost-effective.

96 Post out a post-it shot

This idea is definitely 'out there', but you never know, there might be something in it for you. Picture this:

> A businessperson recently told me about an unusual piece of direct mail he had received in the post. He was sifting through the morning mail, deciding which ones to open first, when a particular envelope attracted his attention. It was a plain brown envelope, handwritten and stamped. When he opened it up, it seemed someone he knew whose name started with the initial 'M' had taken the trouble to send him a photocopy of a magazine advertisement for a product in which he was interested. Well, as you can imagine, he racked his brains trying to work out who this

> mysterious person 'M' actually was, so he could telephone to say thanks. In fact, he even went so far as to retrieve the envelope from the waste bin in the hope that the postmark would give him a clue! The point is he certainly took the time to read carefully through the ad.

Now let me ask you, how would you like your prospects to spend as much time reading through your advertisement? Here's what you do. First, construct a list of mail shot targets and make sure you've got the full name and address of each one. Next, run off black and white photocopies of your current advertisement and don't worry too much about copy quality. Then hand write a message on a small yellow post-it note which simply reads: 'thought you'd be interested in this ...', sign it with your initial and stick in on the bottom left hand corner of your ad. Finally, post out a copy to each of your target respondents in an ordinary, handwritten, stamped, addressed envelope so it just looks like a friend has hurriedly popped it in the post, especially for your prospect. Cheeky, isn't it?

97 Use the discount pack method

Imagine one day you receive a large envelope in the mail. Printed on the envelope, in big bright letters, it says 'Your complimentary discount pack from five of the leading suppliers in your industry'. Curiously, you open up the envelope and inside you find there's a pack of five discount vouchers. For example, if you're in the hotel business then the pack may well include special offers from a plumber, an electrician, a security firm, a furnishing company and a dry cleaner. Now let me ask you, if you received a discount pack like this, don't you think you'd be less likely to throw it away than if you'd been targeted separately by each company? I'd say the chances are you'd be much more likely to see it as a service than a nuisance, and you'd probably take the time to flick through the pack and pick out a couple of coupons of particular interest. The best thing about this idea, though, is that sharing the costs with your fellow suppliers means it's also a highly cost-effective form of sales promotion. Here is how to go about it.

Choose four or five non-competing suppliers who serve your target customers with a range of different, but complementary products and services, and with whom you'd be happy to be associated as a co-promoter. Then telephone to invite them to take part in your discount pack mailing, making it clear that all they have to do is send you X number of discount vouchers to include in the pack which, as with all sales promotions, should be time-fused so that their offer doesn't last indefinitely. Always ask for a contribution towards postage costs, and in particular, make the most of this idea by requesting that each of your co-promoters also sends you the names and addresses of their best prospects. It's a great way to build up a hot mailing list for sending out your discount packs.

98 Send out customer-get-customer letters

By sending out a carefully worded letter requesting referrals from each of your best customers, you can quickly generate dozens of highly qualified sales leads together with a ready made personal introduction from the most credible source there is—a satisfied customer.

When drafting your letter, make sure you start off by thanking your customers for their valued custom and then respectfully request the names of anyone they know who might be in the market for your products and services. Most importantly, include a list of memory-jogging questions to get them thinking about who they know. For example, an accountant could ask their clients:

Who do you know who ...
- *has just started a new business?*
- *is always complaining about the size of their tax bills?*
- *is experiencing problems keeping up to date with their accounts?*

Along with your covering letter, attach a separate sheet in the form of a standardised template, so your customers can give you the name and address details of their referrals. A template with enough space for six names and addresses works well because it encourages people to give you more than one. Above all, never risk cheapening your relationship by offering your customers an incentive to help you out. Remember, a satisfied customer is proud of their choice of supplier and is only too happy to pass on referrals. Needless to say, whenever customers are kind enough to respond, always take the time to telephone to say thanks and to check they don't mind you mentioning their name when you make contact with your new prospect.

99 Try doing the lost letter drop

Here's another fun and quirky idea I couldn't resist including. It's a well known fact that, people being people, we're fascinated by each other's personal lives. In short, we just can't resist a bit of gossip, and turning this curiosity to your advantage is what this idea is all about. Here's an example:

> When a new family restaurant opened in a large city suburb, as with any new local business, the main focus of the initial promotional campaign was to make sure that everyone in the neighbourhood knew about it and its location. To this end, the owners used a number of different promotional approaches. However, what worked particularly well was a large-scale leaflet drop, but one with a difference. They called it the 'lost letter' drop because, unlike the usual style of leaflets that most retailers would circulate to every home owner's letterbox, theirs was made up to look like a page missing from a letter that someone had written to a friend. In other words, it wasn't a leaflet at all; and yet it proved to be extremely effective in raising public awareness and attracting new customers into their restaurant to give it a try. To give you a clear picture of exactly what their 'lost letter' looked like, here it is:

> *although Sue was too ill to do anything about it. Anyway, knowing her* [3]
> *I'm sure she'll pull through like she usually does.*
> *Guess what, I read in the paper that a new family restaurant called 'Sommervilles' has just opened, and the food looks really wholesome—just like my Mum used to make. Apparently, Sally and Bob have already been and they reckon it's brilliant because there's something on the menu for everyone and all for a set price. We can't wait to try it!*
> *Jill, did you know about Anne and Steve? Talk about being caught out! Steve came home unexpectedly from his business trip, let himself in the front door, heard a noise, went upstairs, and you'll never*
> *P.T.O.*

As you'll appreciate, it's important to write the letter in an intimate and chatty style, and to hand write it in a legible scrawl that really looks authentic. Your lost letter can be either single or double sided, just as long as it looks like it's part of a longer, five or six page letter that somehow got lost. With regard to the content of your letter, the trick is to start and finish each side with something gossipy because this hooks people in and gets them interested in reading on. This should then leave you a spare paragraph or two in the middle of the page to draw attention to your business and its features and benefits. Once you have finished drafting the letter, duplicate it on a photocopier (or depending on the costs and quantities involved, get it printed) making sure to choose a blue colour which makes it look as though it's been penned by hand. A good tip is also to make your letter about the same size as that of a standard writing pad (photocopier paper can easily be trimmed down to size after it's been through the machine). Finally, arrange for your lost letter to be distributed to everybody's letterbox within targeted residential areas, either as a stand alone item or as an insert within a free newspaper or similar. With a bit of luck, by the time your recipients realise that your letter is a fake (as if they wouldn't!), their curiosity will have already got the better of them and they'll be reading all about you!

100 Post out some repeater shots

The idea of sending out 'repeater shots' can be highly effective because it's based on the time honoured principle of persistence. It relies completely upon the constant bombardment of your prospects with a highly coordinated series of mailing pieces over a 10-week period. Studies show that the more a person is reminded of another person's name, the more they perceive that person as credible. In particular, however, it's a good way of 'getting your foot in the door' with all those prospects who you know do a lot of business with your competitors—the ones you have been trying to sell to for years, but without success.

Sending out repeater shots involves first putting together a shortlist of appropriate prospects, and preparing in advance a series of 10 letters to be mailed out to each prospect, once every week for 10 weeks. Make sure you write to each prospect by name, saying who you are and where you are from, before going on to give them one good reason why they should be doing business with you instead of their existing supplier. That way, over the course of 10 letters, you will have given them 10 different reasons why they should buy from you. It's important that each letter is concise and follows the same format. It should also start off by referring back to your previous letter, and conclude with a call to action. Here's an example of how the call to action might read on each of your letters:

> *Why don't you give us a try? We want your business and we're ready to serve you. Just call or fax us on the above number.*

Make sure you sign each letter personally, in ink, and hand write the envelopes. Then post out each letter on the same day every week for 10 weeks. It is also worth noting that the inclusion of a small gift in each envelope (such as a note pad or a poster) can act as a powerful incentive for prospects to open your letters, and might even get them into the habit of looking forward to their next letter!

(101) Bounce back a special offer to new customers

A 'bounce back' is a piece of direct mail that is sent to a new customer hard on the heels of their purchase, for the specific purpose of offering them a special deal on a complementary product or service. For example, a carpet cleaning company could make an offer of some carpet care products, or a golf shop could make an offer on a new golf bag to go with the new set of clubs. Here's how to do it.

Once a week, compile a name and address list of all those new customers who have just bought something from your company. Then compile a personal thank you letter that also invites them to take advantage of a special offer on another complementary product or service. Time-fuse the offer so it creates a sense of urgency and ask them to take some form of action, such as to fill out a coupon or telephone you for a free demonstration. Rather than being posted out by itself, you could arrange for your bounce back offer to go out with your guarantee card or warranty contract, invoices or receipts. Alternatively, if you want to create an enhanced sense of urgency, you could even send it out by fax. As long as your bounce back offer hits the customer within a few days of their initial purchase, when they are still in a buying frame of mind, it will stand a good chance of success.

(102) Use the market research briefings technique

If you sell to businesses then this idea could work well, especially if you're looking for a way to start up a dialogue with some difficult prospects. A market research briefing is a concise summary of all the latest market research that has been undertaken in your customers' market—which you send to prospects prior to following up with a telephone call. It's a great way to get your name across, and can act as a powerful 'door opener' to talking business. By the way, please don't be put off by the idea of having to collect information; it's free and (usually) easily accessible in the city library.

To compile your market research briefings, visit the city library's business information department and ask the librarian to direct you to all the latest marketing research reports. Review the reports for key information that relates to your customers' market and produce a short summary covering market size, growth trends and future opportunities, including statistics if possible. A simple bullet point format usually works best. Be professional and always quote your sources. Also, make sure that you use an attention-grabbing title and that your company's name features prominently. For example, if your customer manufactures ball bearings, then you could use a title such as:

The Past, Present and Future of the Ball Bearing Industry
A fact sheet compiled for Turner and Sons
by McIntosh Machine Tools Ltd

The market research summary should then be posted out to selected prospects, together with a brief covering letter, and followed up promptly with a telephone call. The covering letter could also tempt prospects with an offer to supply more detailed information free of charge (providing you know it's available). That way, they'll probably be telephoning you. What a great way to start up a dialogue with your new prospective customer!

103 Do an old prospects blitz

If your company is like most, then one of your most valuable business assets is probably collecting dust right now. I'm referring to all those 'dead' prospects files containing the names and addresses of old prospects with whom, for whatever reason, you never did any business. So an old prospects blitz aims to regenerate them by sending out a simple questionnaire designed to find out why. It rekindles a dialogue and hopefully in such a way as to bring them back to life. Here is what you do.

Dig out your dead prospect files and compile a hit list made up of all those you think may have life in them yet. Send them a personalised letter with the key message being: 'We'd like the opportunity to serve you'. Enclose a simple questionnaire, designed to identify their new requirements and to subtly uncover exactly what you have to do to get their business back. Encourage them to complete the questionnaire by enclosing a discount voucher redeemable against their next purchase—so every time a completed questionnaire comes back to you, it means their business is on its way too!

104 Try the sell through technique

Imagine you own a hairdressing salon. You place an advertisement in a glossy magazine at a cost of $900. As a result, you eventually get 15 new customers, so in effect it costs you $60 to 'buy' each of your 15 new customers.

Now picture this. Instead of using traditional advertising, you decide to try a different approach. You telephone a local beauty clinic and tell them you have 200 vouchers for free haircuts. Each voucher is worth the price of the haircut, which is $30. You then go on to explain that you'd like them to send each of their top 200 customers one of your vouchers as a free gift. Of course, the beauty clinic is going to jump at the chance to say thank you to their top customers in this way because, apart from the postage, it isn't going to cost them anything. Meanwhile, you've succeeded in attracting lots of new customers into your salon and with a bit of luck, from now on, most of them will turn into regular customers paying full prices. Granted, you'll have paid a nominal amount to get the voucher printed, plus you'll have incurred the wages cost of delivering the first haircut free—but that's going to be far less than the $60 cost per customer using the more traditional approach of magazine advertising.

The concept of offering a free gift of some description to a host company or organisation as a means of doing a 'sell through' their customer base is one which can be made to work for many different types of businesses. The free gift could be a $10 gift voucher, a free service, free product or a free consultation—it really doesn't matter, providing you choose an appropriate host company that will benefit by being able to offer your gift as a thank you to their most valued customers.

105 Use the crumpled postcard flyer

For a really whacky idea, try this one on for size! Michelle, a top real estate salesperson, once explained to me how she uses this idea as a means of generating more than her fair share of property listings. She goes to her local stationers and buys 250 envelopes together with 750 postage stamps, a post-it note pad, some blue carbon paper and a pack of 500 plain white flimsy postcards. She also hand writes a few lines to go on the postcard and asks the stationers to turn it into a rubber stamp. This means that, by using the rubber stamp together with a blue ink pad, at first sight it looks just like a handwritten note, yet it can be reproduced in a fraction of the time. The note reads:

Thinking of selling your home?
Want top dollar?
For a free, no-obligation appraisal call me on XXXX XXXX.
Thanks, Michelle

Armed with a name and address list of 250 selected home owners, the second stage of the operation involves preparing two identical postcards which will be mailed out on two separate occasions to the 250 home owners. Obviously, by using the rubber stamp, together with the carbon paper to write the names and addresses, Michelle saves a lot of time, but it also enables her to produce two postcards for each home owner which are virtually identical to one another in every respect.

The next stage of the operation is when Michelle posts out one postcard to each home owner—the first 250 postcards. According to Michelle, what happens next is highly predictable: the home owners receive the postcard but, because it is so plain and boring, almost all of them end up getting thrown away, straight into the dustbin. At this point, however, Michelle gets to work on the second, follow-up mailout. This involves using the remaining 250 postcards, envelopes, stamps and post-it notes. You see, the next mailing the home owners receive from Michelle (a few days after having received their postcard) is a handwritten, stamped addressed envelope. Inside the envelope is what looks like their original postcard, because it has been crumpled up and then flattened out again. Stuck to the bottom of the crumpled postcard is a yellow post-it note that reads:

Please don't throw this out again!
Call me.
Michelle

What a clever promotion! Not only is this approach simple and relatively inexpensive, but it also has the added advantage of having that indefinable 'X factor' that really gets you noticed. You can just imagine the startled home owners wondering, if only for a brief moment, if Michelle really had taken the trouble to search through their dustbins to retrieve their postcard. Could you use a similar approach in your business?

106 Email an email shot

By far the most popular use of the Internet the world over is the sending and receiving of email messages. Let's face it, for most businesspeople, this means the use of email as a direct marketing tool is surely destined to become the 'medium of choice'. Watch this space! Certainly, an email-based promotional campaign lends itself to just about every type of business, because it offers the opportunity to communicate a specific offer in a highly cost-effective, quick, targeted and personalised way. Here's a checklist to help you to get started with using this ultra-powerful marketing tool:

1 The sending of unsolicited messages on the Internet is generally seen as an invasion of privacy. So when you gain a new customer or inquirer, along with your request for their email address, always ask for their permission to send your promotional emails. Then, as a part of every promotional email you send, make a point of reminding recipients of this fact as well as giving them an opportunity to opt out of your emailing program if they so desire.

2 Just like a conventional mailing program, pay special attention to your mailing list, which should be made up of customers who are in your target market and who are ready and willing to hear from you. Be warned; poorly targeted email shots not only fail miserably but also tend to have the effect of seriously undermining a firm's reputation in the marketplace.

3 Like a telephone call, time your email shot to arrive on screen at a time most suitable to your customers.

4 Remember to include an email 'signature' at the end of each message. This is the equivalent of your company letterhead on your stationery, and should include your name, company, position, web site address, telephone and fax numbers and physical address.

5 When sending out the same message to a list of email addresses 'en masse', be sure to use the blind carbon copy facility (BCC), so that recipients cannot access your entire mailing list.

6 Include a benefit loaded 'header' (subject line) because that's what your recipient will see first. An email header has to grab your recipient's attention or it will be deleted within an instant!

7 With regard to the content of your email shot, it's important that your proposition to customers represents some kind of special offer that runs for a limited time only. Personalise your message, keep it short and sharp, and always include a call to action.

IDEAS FOR BECOMING AN
EXPERT SALES PROSPECTOR

The term 'sales prospecting' refers to a systematic approach to identifying potential customers using a variety of methods that rely purely on the individual efforts of the businessperson.

Owner–managers of successful small businesses make the most of a wide range of sales prospecting methods to generate a constant stream of high quality, low cost sales leads.

Sales prospecting only
works when you do.

Do some piggyback trade show prospecting

Trade shows are, at least potentially, a good source of sales leads because they usually attract large numbers of prospects who all congregate under the same roof for a short period of time.

There are a number of ways to approach the task of prospecting at a trade show. You could, of course, rent some space in the exhibition hall and set up a stand. This can be quite expensive though, and there is always a temptation to spend more money than you would like on fixtures and fittings, especially if your stand is going to be competing directly with those of your major competitors.

An alternative approach, however, is to strike a deal with one of your counterparts who sells non-competing products or services to your target customers, and who is going to be exhibiting at your trade show. Offer to provide them with an additional attraction for customers to visit their stand in the form of a small cardboard postbox to be placed on their desk or counter area. The idea is that you offer one of your company's products (providing this is feasible) in a free prize draw and that you clearly advertise this on the box. All people have to do is post their business card (or name and address details) in your box and they automatically go into the draw. Obviously, the beauty of this 'piggybacking' approach is that your host company gets the benefit of additional traffic at their stand while you get the benefit of the names and addresses of plenty of new potential customers.

Ask for a referral with every customer you meet

After every sales visit, regardless of the outcome, if you can acquire the habit of asking a simple question just before you leave, you will be able to maintain a constant flow of high quality sales leads. Here it is:

> Tell me, Jim, if we swapped jobs right now, and you were in my shoes, who would you go to see next?

It may well seem like an obvious question to ask, but it's one that most businesspeople have a tendency to forget. Yet providing it is asked in the right spirit, it's amazing how most people will want to help you out. Probe for as much background information as you can about your new prospect, in addition to getting their contact details. What's more, always remember to check that it is okay for you to mention your informant's name when you make contact. Obviously, any new prospect is going to be a lot more receptive if you can introduce yourself by saying that someone they know gave you their name and address.

109 Arrange a breakfast focus group

Do you have any of those really difficult prospects—the ones that seem to be 'owned' by your competitors—the ones you've been trying to do business with for years, but never seem to be able to get a look in? Well if so, here's an idea that might just help you start up a dialogue with them. It's the simple idea of inviting them to attend a breakfast focus group meeting, so they can tell you what you have to do in order to be in with a chance of getting their business. Here is what you do.

First, plan to invite no more than about four or five selected target buyers, and arrange for the breakfast to be held in a private room of a top hotel. Second, send out personal invitations and be sure to make it absolutely clear that the breakfast is completely free, and that there will be no hard sell. Just explain that you'd like to give them the opportunity of making a personal contact in your company, as well as with some other influential businesspeople from other companies within their industry. Third, within a day or two, follow up your invitation with a telephone call to see if they're coming. With a bit of luck you'll at least be put through to speak with your prospect because they will feel obligated to reply to your kind invitation. Needless to say, if necessary, use this call as an opportunity to persuade them to come. This can usually be done by putting the focus on the breakfast itself, because the thought of a full silver service breakfast always seems to work well as a drawcard for businesspeople!

110 Woo them with a wooing survey

Have you ever been approached by a sales representative from a security company, selling burglar alarms and offering to do a free security appraisal of your place of business? I was, and when I said yes I was amazed at how professionally I was handled. Not only did the salesperson conduct a detailed survey, which must have taken a full half-hour, but it was also followed up with a beautifully written and extremely useful report which outlined a number of weaknesses in our security system. Well that's a classic example of a 'wooing survey' because it's a means of starting a dialogue with a prospective customer and exposing their needs but without doing a hard sell. Here's what to do.

Think about the ways in which you could assess your customer's problems, with a view to offering them a free diagnosis of their situation together with a written report of your findings. Reassure your customers that by undergoing your survey they're under absolutely no obligation to buy. Then, in the report itself, recommend solutions to problems, not products. For example, the security firm I referred to earlier recommended total peace of mind, not burglar alarms. Above all, make your report objective, but at the same time seize every opportunity you can to let them glimpse just how good things really could be if they went ahead and took advantage of your product or service offer.

111 Always be on dictaphone duty

One of my favourite expressions goes like this:

> Good salespeople are like policeman—because they're always on duty!

In other words, regardless of whether they are driving down the motorway, walking around town, at a conference or trade exhibition, or simply at home watching TV, good salespeople are constantly on the lookout for new leads, wherever they are and whatever they are doing (well almost!). Of course, this simply means being alert to all sorts of potentially useful bits of everyday information—such as a new office block being built, a news item on the radio or someone mentioning the name of a new company in the area, that kind of thing. So how should you go about capturing this kind of information? Well, I am convinced that by far the most convenient and practical way is to use a pocket dictaphone. Keeping one handy throughout the day means you can record the details of each lead on the spot, just like a policeman! By arranging to have your tapes typed up, say once a week, you can then act on them on a regular basis.

112 Use the networking memory jogger

Stored away in the minds of our friends and colleagues are literally dozens of ready qualified sales leads, and a useful method of unlocking this valuable information is to use a memory jogger. I'm talking about using a simple list of questions designed to help people remember the names of all their old and existing contacts. In fact, the great thing about using a memory jogger is that people tend to enjoy the process of remembering who they know, which means you can easily end up with a surprisingly large number of names and addresses.

When constructing a memory jogger, the key thing is that it should be specifically designed to help someone remember all those people they know and who could be in the market for your products and services. For example, the real estate salesperson's memory jogger would include questions such as:

- *Who do you know who may be thinking of selling their home?*

- *Who do you know who's renting at the moment, but who may want to buy their own house soon?*

- *Who do you know who's shortly going to be re-locating?*

- *Who do you know who's going to get married soon?*

Get the idea? Obviously it's important to include as many questions as you possibly can in order to jog someone's memory from every conceivable angle. Then, once you've finalised your memory jogger, go and see everyone you know who you think might be able to help. Meet them for a coffee and go through the memory jogger, question by question. Make sure you gather as much information as you can and don't forget to check that it's okay for you to mention their name when you make contact with your new prospect.

113 Get into viral marketing

Viral marketing occurs when people tell other people about you and the word spreads, just like a real virus, throughout a population. Consequently, getting into viral marketing simply involves doing all you can to get people to recommend you and pass on your sales message to family members, friends, associates and others in their network. One of the best ways of doing this is via the Internet. Here's a great example:

> Since its launch in 1996, the email delivery system 'Hotmail' is reputed to have grown a worldwide customer base of tens of millions of people, with many thousands of new users signing up every day. Yet apparently, this phenomenal growth has been achieved with an extremely small promotional budget. How did they do it? Viral marketing. Cleverly, the key

to their success was to ensure that every time a user sent an email message to a friend or associate, the recipient also received a brief advertising message encouraging them to sign up with Hotmail. This meant that, in effect, every single user of the Hotmail system became a salesperson for the company, helping to spread their sales message around the globe like wildfire!

Needless to say, unless you're a free email provider you're probably not going to be able to utilise the Internet in quite the same way as Hotmail. Nevertheless, there are lots of other ways to use the Internet for the purpose of viral marketing. Some of these are as follows. You could:

- *include a 'P.S. Please pass this on …' message when sending out promotional emails to customers and prospects, or when you're sending an enewsletter to subscribers*

- *develop a company screensaver that people can download from your web site and pass on to others*

- *encourage other companies to link their web site to yours, especially your suppliers and those selling non-competing products and services into your market*

- *add a 'send this page to a friend' link at the bottom of your web site pages.*

Of course, beyond the Internet, there are plenty of other approaches to viral marketing that you could employ, limited only by your imagination. For example, you could:

- *provide a forum of some kind for your customers to tell other people about you*

- *tell your customers true stories about anything humorous, fascinating or amazing that has happened in your business; something that's guaranteed to capture their imagination and that they'll want to tell other people about*

- *supply fully stocked business card or leaflet dispensers to be located in the reception areas of any business that can recommend you, such as your accountant, business advisor, health care practitioner, hairdresser, or whoever.*

As you can see, viral marketing is a great concept, and it can be extremely effective in spreading the word and generating fresh business. All you have to do is jump into the driving seat and make it happen in any and every way you can.

114 Build a network of influential contacts

Other salespeople selling non-competing products and services into the same marketplace can provide you with a fertile source of new sales leads. So it is well worth making a point of getting to know your counterparts and cultivating a network of useful contacts in your industry. All you have to do is meet on a regular basis and swap information. Notably, your contacts do not need to be restricted to other salespeople—other influential people such as business advisers, management consultants and accountants can be equally as useful. It's an old cliché, but when it comes to generating new business, it's not what you know, but who you know that makes the biggest difference to your sales figures.

115 Become a regular public speaker

Research into people's innermost fears has revealed that, apparently, people are more frightened of public speaking than they are of dying! Whether this is true or not, it certainly highlights the fact that most people are very nervous about public speaking, which is why this idea can really set you apart from the rest. Unlike the vast majority of mediocre salespeople, the top performers generate tremendous amounts of new business simply by being prepared to offer their services as a guest speaker at any type of gathering where their target customers are likely to be. For example, at chambers of commerce meetings, business club meetings, trade federation meetings and so on. Why not do likewise? Providing your talk is generally informative and interesting to your audience (make sure you do not do a hard sell), you are bound to get spin-off benefits in the form of sales leads.

116 Harness scrapbook power

Most businesspeople spend so much time out of the office, they simply do not have enough time to read through all the trade journals to which they subscribe. This is unfortunate, given that trade journals often contain valuable sales leads. For example, many news items relate to useful customer information, such as details of small companies starting up a new business in your area, or larger companies expanding into new locations.

One way of making the most of this rich source of leads is to arrange for office-bound staff to scan the trade press on a regular basis, with a view to 'cutting and pasting' any useful looking articles into a scrapbook. If necessary, this information could even be sorted by sales territory or by product type, depending on how your salespeople are organised. The key advantage of this idea is that it provides salespeople with a central source of ready sorted sales leads that otherwise would have been missed.

117 Search your local library for sales leads

There are many useful prospect sources in the business section of your local city library that are free and readily available. The main ones include business directories (those which are industry specific and usually published annually), trade publications (such as journals and magazines, membership directories and year books) and government publications (for example, details of planning permissions, which may be a good source of leads for builders, furnishers, office suppliers, etc.). In addition, most libraries also have access to online databases providing detailed company information.

Searching your local library for sales leads may not sound as exciting as some other forms of lead identification but it can be a surprisingly good source. For the sake of a small investment of time and effort, the local library is usually well worth a visit.

118 Conduct lead-generating competitions among staff

In most companies, the only staff charged with the responsibility of generating sales leads are salespeople. However, there is no reason why other members of staff should not be encouraged to take part in your company's lead-generating activities. Just because someone works in accounts, administration or production doesn't mean they do not have friends, relatives or other associates who may be interested (or know someone who may be interested) in learning more about your products and services.

One of the best ways to generate new sales leads from non-sales staff is to run a competition from time to time. Here's how to go about it.

First, this kind of competition should always be run over a limited time period, so it really focuses people's efforts. Second, make it clear that it is purely voluntary and open to everyone in the company. By giving the competition a code name such as 'Project X', this will help capture people's imaginations and get them interested in taking part. Third, design a special entry form for staff to fill out with the contact details of each sales lead they come up with, together with a brief note as to the source of the lead. Distribute plenty of entry forms and be sure to arm your staff with any sales literature they may need, including business cards if necessary. Fourth, keep a 'league table' showing how many leads each member of staff has generated, with a grand prize offer for the top producer and lots of fun prizes for everyone else who takes part.

119 Use the appointment-getting close

When you are in a face-to-face selling situation, here's how to turn one difficult prospect into two sales. When being pressed for discount by a tough buyer, don't give the discount, trade it for something which costs your customer nothing but which is priceless to you—a booked appointment with another genuine prospect. Here's how to do it.

During the early stages of the sale, check out the prospect's ability to refer you on to other genuine prospects. For maximum effect, set up this close by making sure that you have maintained a tough negotiating position throughout the sale. Then when they absolutely, positively won't budge on terms, put a glint in your eye and say something like this:

> Okay Jim, I'll tell you what … if you can set me up with an appointment with another genuine prospective customer right now, then I'll go along with your terms. There's the telephone!

120 Set up a voucher partnership

Here's an imaginative method by which two companies can form a partnership to their mutual advantage. Whenever a customer makes a purchase from either company, both your salespeople and your partner's salespeople hand over a special discount voucher redeemable against their next purchase from the *other* company. For example, new customers to a gym could be offered vouchers redeemable for sports equipment purchased at a local sports shop, and vice versa. This idea attracts lots of new customers for both partners and is also a highly credible way to endorse the superior quality of each other's products and services.

Choose a partnership with a reputable company of roughly equal size that sells complementary and non-competing products and services into your market. Arrange to share the cost of printing some discount vouchers. On the voucher, clearly explain that it entitles all customers of either business to a discount of $X off their next purchase of the other company's products and services. Also be sure to specify any conditions of purchase. For example, you and your partner might decide that the vouchers should only be valid for purchases over a certain amount. Most importantly, as with all such promotions, make sure your vouchers are time-fused by including an 'offer ends by …' date. Finally, instruct all salespeople that, at the point of sale, the voucher is to be handed out as a means of thanking a customer for making their purchase, and as an encouragement for them to shop with your company and your partner's company once again during the period of your promotion.

121 Post out a mystery tape

When you've tried absolutely everything you know to book an appointment with an important buyer but you just can't get past the secretary, try posting out a mystery cassette tape and you'll be guaranteed their personal and undivided attention. Here's what to do.

When recording your message, start by introducing yourself and congratulating your prospective customer on having an excellent secretary, explaining straight away the reason why you've had to resort to sending them a taped message! Keep your message very brief and very friendly, selling only the appointment and its benefit to your prospect. It is most important that you do not attempt to sell your product or service on the tape—the only time you should do that is when you get to meet the prospect face-to-face. Then at the end of your message request that, the next time you telephone, they instruct their secretary to put you through. Finally, post out the tape 'incognito', in a blank envelope and marked 'private and confidential', with no visible clue as to where or who it has come from or what it's about. It's a cheeky but irresistible formula because, even if this idea doesn't get you an appointment, at least your prospect will never forget you!

122 Do an after hours voice-mail blitz

If you sell business-to-business, then you've probably already got the telephone numbers of a long list of hot prospects who you've tried to ring, but for one reason or another you've just not been able to get through. Well if that's the case, why not try doing an after hours voice-mail blitz? By leaving a well scripted message on their answerphone late in the evening, it's often quite surprising just how many prospects will be sufficiently impressed to return your call the next day.

When leaving your message, start off by saying who you are and explaining that you've been trying to get hold of them for a while. Then tell them that the reason why you're ringing at such and such a time (make a special point of mentioning the time) is in the hope that you might have caught them working late. Next, go on to say that you'd like to talk to them about something that you feel would be of great benefit to their business, and that you would appreciate a return call. Conclude the call by leaving your name and number. Speak slowly, and repeat your name and number again before hanging up. Always remember, though, that the most important thing about your telephone message is the way you sound. Pay special attention to the tone, pitch and pronunciation of your message so that you come across in the right way.

(123) Use Alastair's magic cold-calling card method

For many years, Alastair has sold an electricity saving device to manufacturing companies, and with great success. According to Alastair, the single most important part of his job is the ability to prospect for new potential customers and get to see key decision makers, usually the factory manager or the production director. So when I asked how he went about the task of sales prospecting, I was quite surprised when he told me that he still did most of it the old fashioned way by knocking on doors— otherwise known as 'cold calling'. I was surprised because these days, fewer and fewer buyers will agree to see a salesperson on the spot without an appointment. If you try, typically (but not always) the receptionist will give you the name of the person you need to see and take your business card, but that's about as far as you'll get! That's why I was fascinated to hear about Alastair's technique, which goes something like this.

Alastair greets the receptionist, introduces himself, and asks who in the factory or manufacturing plant is responsible for buying. Having got the name of the person he needs to see, he then writes it down across the top of one of his special cold-calling cards. Next, he hands the card to the receptionist and asks if they would be kind enough to go and give it to the buyer. Here's a copy of the card:

Good Day _____

Mins   Secs

[0][0] : [2][5]

... IS ALL I NEED OF YOUR
VALUABLE TIME!

I promise I am not going to talk about
get-rich-quick schemes or religion ...

IN FACT, I'M NOT GOING
TO TALK AT ALL!

But what you will experience
could well save you a
lot of money, starting today.

Rest assured 25 seconds
is all it will take.

Will you see me?
Alastair

Alastair was quick to point out that, although not all receptionists will oblige, most of them will because they're keen to find out what's involved. Likewise, although not all buyers will agree to see you, he claims that most of them will because their curiosity usually gets the better of them too! Oh, and by the way, whenever Alastair does get to meet up with a buyer, he always keeps his word and says nothing. Instead, he gets a mini-cassette player out of his briefcase and plays a 25-second pre-recorded tape which features one of his customers explaining why it would be well worth the buyer investing another 15 minutes of their time finding out all about what Alastair has to offer! Could you use a similar approach?

(124) Issue introductory discount cards

If you'd like to motivate and encourage all staff members to get involved in finding new customers for your business, then an 'introductory discount card' scheme is one of the best ways of going about it. It works like this.

For a limited period (say for six weeks of the year when business is normally a little slow), issue each of your staff with a limited number of introductory discount cards (say six per employee). The card then gives your staff the authority to introduce new VIP customers to your business—VIPs such as their family members, friends and acquaintances—and at a specially discounted rate. All your staff have to do is issue the card to selected individuals of their choice, authorising the discount by signing the card. Then all the new customer has to do to take advantage of the offer is to present the card to your salesperson when making their first purchase.

When organising your introductory discount card scheme, by far the most important factor is the actual card itself, which must give the impression of being of what it is—a rare, valuable and highly sought-after item that a new customer is lucky enough to have given to them by one of your staff members. So make sure it's produced on a high quality gold or silver coloured card, and well designed. On the card, highlight the fact that it entitles the bearer to special savings, and state clearly the date by which the offer expires. Most importantly, include a space for the employee's signature. Using their signature as a means of authorising the offer not only makes your employee feel special, but it also has the effect of personalising the relationship between your company and your new customer. The other key aspects of running a successful introductory discount card scheme are as follows:

- *Run the scheme on a voluntary basis only.*

- *Make it clear that the cards are to be handed out to new customers only and that the distribution of the cards must be done in the employees' own time.*

- *Ensure your scheme runs for a limited period and that it is promoted as an exclusive, once-a-year-only offer.*

125 Confirm every sales appointment with a PS letter

Have you ever gone to an appointment that you had originally made by telephone, only to find that when you get there, the prospect is unavailable because they had forgotten about it? If so, then you'll already know how frustrating it is (not to mention a complete waste of time)! Worse still, this situation presents a real dilemma because, on the one hand, we know we really ought to telephone the day before, just to make sure our prospective customer is still expecting us; yet on the other hand, in so doing, we're inviting rejection. That's why I always make a point of confirming every sales appointment by letter, straight away. Nothing elaborate, just a simple letter saying 'further to our telephone conversation, I look forward to meeting you on such and such a date, at such and such a time, yours sincerely'. However, the crucial part of the letter is the 'PS'. I always add a PS to the bottom of the letter that says:

> *If this appointment is no longer convenient, please get back to me immediately. Otherwise, I'll see you on the 12th.*

I find there are two advantages to sending out a PS letter like this. First, the letter itself serves as a permanent reminder of the date and time of the appointment. Secondly, as time goes by and the appointment draws near, the PS makes it more difficult for the prospect to back out because, providing they did not respond immediately, then this has the effect of obligating them to see you as planned.

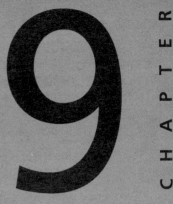

IDEAS FOR CLOSING
MORE SALES FACE-TO-FACE

Effective face-to-face selling involves the use of a wide range of persuasion and interpersonal communication skills for the purpose of making sales.

Owner–managers of successful small businesses perform an important role as salespeople. They know how to sell, and they know how to do it professionally.

When all is said and done,
nothing happens in a
business until someone
sells something.

Adopt a customer-oriented selling approach

There are two philosophies of personal selling. The old, traditional philosophy takes the view that the most important thing is to make the sale. This is the sales-oriented selling approach, which emphasises the ability of the salesperson to 'close the sale' (gain the customer's agreement) above all else. By contrast, the modern philosophy takes the view that the most important thing is to satisfy the customer. This is the customer-oriented approach, which highlights the need for the salesperson to see the sale not as an end in itself (as a one-off transaction), but rather as just the beginning of a potentially long and mutually beneficial business relationship. To put it another way, whereas the sales-oriented approach emphasises the needs of the salesperson and focuses on a short-term pay-off, the customer-oriented approach emphasises the needs of the customer and focuses on a longer-term pay-off. The list below contrasts the modern, professional customer-oriented approach to selling with the old-fashioned notion of the fast-talking manipulative salesperson:

Sales-oriented selling	versus	Customer-oriented selling
I win/you lose	v.	I win/you win
Manipulative	v.	Persuasive
'I sold it'	v.	'You bought it'
Short-term focus	v.	Long-term focus

In an increasingly competitive business world, the old-fashioned, sales-oriented approach is quite simply no longer appropriate. Modern professional selling is about the ability to create a satisfied customer, build referrals and secure repeat sales. It's all a question of attitude. The choice is yours.

 ## Prepare for every sales visit

Once when Lee Trevino, the great American golfer, was asked to comment on the good luck he had one day when playing in a competition, he is reputed to have said to the interviewer:

You know, the funny thing is, the harder I practise, the luckier I get!

Of course, you could say the same thing about selling—the more effort you put into preparing for every sale before you go in, the better you will perform in front of the customer and the more sales you will make. To a large extent, it all comes down to good old-fashioned preparation.

Assuming you already have the necessary knowledge about your products, your competitors and your industry, then effective preparation for each sales visit is the name of the game. It need not take long. In most cases it is simply a matter of focusing your mind on five key questions:

1 What is my primary objective for this sales visit (for example, is it to make a sale, secure a trial order, arrange a demonstration or what)?

2 If, for whatever reason, I cannot achieve my primary objective, what is my next best, secondary or fall back objective?

3 What are likely to be the particular individual requirements of this customer, and how can I best satisfy them?

4 Who is this customer likely to see as being my main competitor, and why should they buy from me instead of them?

5 Why might this customer consider not buying from me, and how can I best handle these objections?

128 Make a mental movie of your next sale

By drawing on the databanks of your memory, within a few split seconds you can make a 'mental movie' of any one of tens of thousands of past experiences, in such detail that you can quite literally re-live that experience inside your head. Now imagine that, instead of making a mental movie of the past, you make one of the future—a movie relating to the next sale that you have to make. That's when making a mental movie can really work for you. By projecting a future sales scenario onto the screen of your mind and making a movie of it, you can 'live out' the experience just as you want it to happen, thereby effectively conditioning yourself for a successful outcome. It's a three-step process.

First, visualise yourself successfully acting out your part as the consummate professional salesperson, and in great detail. Second, add the sound track, so that you can hear inside your head every single piece of the dialogue between you and your customer, just in the way you want it to unfold. Third, add the emotion, so that you can really feel the sense of elation and success you're going to experience as you visualise the sale moving along towards your desired outcome, culminating in the customer making a positive purchase decision. This kind of mental movie making process has been used by top salespeople for many years. If it works for them, it can work for you. Try it!

(129) Control your self-talk

Do you talk to yourself? If, when you read that question, you heard a little voice inside your head saying: 'Do I talk to myself? No, I don't do that …', then of course the answer is yes, you do talk to yourself! But don't worry, it's perfectly normal. We all talk to ourselves, and psychologists even have a term for it. They call it 'self-talk'.

The interesting thing about self-talk is that, unless we make a conscious effort to control it and make it work for us, it usually ends up working against us. In other words, we often allow ourselves to slip into negative self-talk, effectively conditioning ourselves to end up getting all those things we don't want, instead of those things we do want. By means of an example, cast your mind back to the last time you had an important but difficult sales presentation lined up. In those last critical moments before you actually met the buyer, perhaps you allowed your little voice to say things like 'our price is too expensive' or 'I know I'm wasting my time on this one'. See what I mean? So make an effort to become more aware of your self-talk from now on. Take control of it and start talking to yourself in a more positive way. If you can get into the habit of using your inner voice to your advantage, you'll be programming yourself to be more successful more often.

(130) Do the handshake 1–2–3

The 'handshake 1–2–3' is one of the most important techniques to learn and to master for any salesperson operating in a business setting where a handshake is the usual form of greeting between a buyer and seller. It's important because a handshake normally occurs within the first few seconds of a meeting, when the customer is still forming their first impressions of the salesperson and (by association) their company. As the saying goes:

In selling, you never get a second chance to make a good first impression!

Doing the handshake 1–2–3 is an excellent habit to acquire, because it means you will always be making the most of the opportunity a handshake presents for creating a favourable first impression, and building some rapport with your customer. As the term implies, when shaking hands, there are three things to remember. First, always look the customer directly in the eye, and in such a way that, albeit briefly, you look right into the pupils of their eyes. At this moment a powerful human bonding process takes place which, according to experts, can have a profound effect on the way people instinctively relate to one another from then on. Second, smile! For goodness sake, show your customer that you're happy to meet them, and that when you're saying 'pleased to meet you' you actually look like you really mean it! Third, make sure you shake hands with a straight, firm grip that's neither too firm nor too limp. Above all, avoid the tendency to try to dominate a handshake either by shaking too vigorously and for too long, or by tilting and rolling your hand so that it's over the top of your customer's hand. A straight, firm handshake says a lot about who you are and your attitude to the customer.

(131) Set an agenda

Let's say you have just met up with your new prospective customer, you've introduced yourself and made a good first impression. Next, you've been through the ritual of chatting a little and have taken the opportunity of building some rapport between you. So now what? Well, now is the time to take control of the conversation by providing the customer with a 'road map' of how you intend to proceed. In other words, you should suggest an outline agenda for the meeting and get the customer's agreement to it so that you can get started in a businesslike way. Nothing too elaborate. Simply say you'd like to cover this, then that, and so on, in order to make the best use of your time together. For example, you could say something like this:

> I'd like to start by taking a few minutes to tell you a little about myself and my company. Next, I want to spend as much time as it takes to find out all about you and your requirements. Then I'd like to explain exactly how I think we could help … okay?

Adopting this approach has a number of advantages. Not only does it come across as being professional, but more importantly, it provides you with an element of control throughout the rest of the meeting, so that whenever necessary you are able to refer back to it and move things along to the next stage.

Make good use of the customer's name

People enjoy hearing the sound of their own name because it is distinctly personal. Indeed, in an increasingly impersonal world, perhaps it's true to say that, in business these days, using someone's name, remembering it and getting it right are more important that ever before. Certainly when all is said and done, people do business with people, not departments, companies or markets! Think for a moment about the way the use of someone's name can actually change the feel of a question. For example, consider the difference between a question phrased like this:

Now let me ask you, when do you think ...

and one phrased like this:

Now Jim, let me ask you, when do you think ...

There's only a little word change, but there's a big difference in the feel of the way the question is being asked, wouldn't you agree? This is why it is so important to pay special attention to your use of someone's name and to become a truly 'professional' name user. To do so, you'll need to develop the following habits.

When meeting someone for the first time, listen carefully to their name and make a note of it. If it is an unusual name, check to see that you have got it right and, if necessary, ask them to spell it for you. Remember, getting someone's name wrong is far worse than not using it at all! Then, as soon as it is appropriate to do so, ask if you can call them by their first name. Make a point of using it to personalise the rest of the conversation and as a means of helping to build a friendly rapport between you.

 ## Understand the language of silent selling

Face-to-face communication always has two components—the audible and the inaudible. The audible component relates to what people say, the words they use and how they say them. It is the spoken language of communication. The inaudible component, on the other hand, relates to the unspoken 'silent' messages conveyed through the body language of movements, postures and gestures. Although body language is by no means a perfect science (in the sense that it is often open to various interpretations), there are nonetheless a number of simple applications which salespeople should learn to master in order to enhance their communication skills.

As a salesperson, you can convey openness, enthusiasm and cooperation by ensuring your jacket or coat is unbuttoned, by smiling frequently, maintaining an upright upper body posture with open hands, making plenty of direct eye contact, and by always sitting on the edge of your chair rather than slouching! When the customer is talking, it is also important to show them that you are closely evaluating what they are saying. This can be achieved by nodding periodically, slightly tilting your head, making notes, stroking your chin, peering over your glasses, or even taking your glasses off and holding them in a thoughtful manner.

Apart from being aware of your own body language and the signals you are conveying, you also need to look out for the signals being communicated by your customer. In particular, you will need to stay alert to any sign of defensiveness or suspicion such as crossed arms, crossed legs, clenched hands, hands in pockets or fidgeting. In these circumstances, your overriding objective is to try and put your customer at ease and defuse the tension. On a more positive note, you should also be aware of any body language which suggests the buyer is in the process of deciding to buy! 'Silent buying signals' occur—for example, when the customer picks up the contract for a closer look, inspects the product more clearly, nods and smiles in agreement to a key selling point, or gradually becomes more open and relaxed-looking.

134 Take the time to interview your customer

If there is one characteristic shared by most buyers, it is their need to feel that the salesperson thoroughly understands their situation. Professional salespeople always appreciate this and take their time to question, clarify and probe the customer's needs, problems and solution areas. By contrast, inexperienced salespeople often have a tendency to rush things, which can easily be misinterpreted in a negative way by the buyer. At best, the rushed salesperson is likely to be seen as insensitive to their particular buying situation. Worse still, it could even be viewed as an attempt to cover up some kind of weakness in the salesperson's offer. Consequently, when interviewing the customer, always take the time to do it properly, and take some advice from Rudyard Kipling:

> *I keep six serving men, they taught me all I knew*
> *Their names are What and Why, and When*
> *and How and Where and Who!*

Early on in your sales presentation, make a point of asking plenty of these kinds of open questions, beginning with the words 'what', 'where', 'when', 'how', 'who' and 'why'. Resolve to become an expert interviewer and really get your customer talking, because nothing arouses someone's interest more than when they're talking about themselves, their business, their problems and their solutions.

135 Trigger your customer's imagination

Cast your mind back to the last time you made a major purchase of some kind, perhaps a decision to buy a new home or to go on the holiday of a lifetime. Now ask yourself this: in finally making up your mind to proceed with the purchase, isn't it true that you allowed yourself the luxury of thinking ahead and imagining just how good you would feel once you owned that new home, or were actually on that holiday? Of course you did! Which is why one of the key skills of professional selling is the ability to help customers engage their own imagination.

In triggering your customer's imagination, the key is to ask them to step out of reality and be creative. Here are some examples showing the types of words and phrases you can use.

Example 1
Imagine the machine had been up and running in your factory since the start of the year—in what ways do you think you'd have benefited from it so far? (gets the customer to imagine a different past)
Example 2
Just pretend the service is already in place right now—what unnecessary functions would it eliminate for you and your staff? (gets the customer to imagine a different present)
Example 3
Let's say it's the end of the financial year and you've actually achieved your projected sales figure. Tell me what would that mean to you in terms of …? (gets the customer to imagine a different future)

The fact is, when customers assume ownership of a product or service they begin to live out the benefits in the theatre of their mind—a place which is full of the possibilities about how good life could be, once they've made the decision to buy. So as you can see, the trick is to ask questions that encourage customers to imagine a world in which they already own your product or service, because as soon as they do that, then your job becomes a whole lot easier!

136 Become an expert listener

The flip side of asking questions is listening to the answers given. In fact, listening actively (showing that you are listening) rather than passively (deadpan response) is every bit as important as asking questions.

The key to becoming an expert listener is to appreciate that there is a big difference between listening and waiting for your turn to speak. Being a good listener means showing an interest in what's being said, and it is a basic skill that all salespeople should learn to master because when someone is talking about themselves and their business, to them it is the most important subject under the sun. Furthermore, it demonstrates concern, builds trust, helps reduce sales resistance and, most importantly, turns you into a brilliant conversationalist. Consider the following quotation:

> *People who talk about other people are gossips,*
> *people who talk about themselves are boring,*
> *but people who talk about me are brilliant conversationalists!*

Listening actively is when you use the following techniques to show the customer that you are listening carefully:

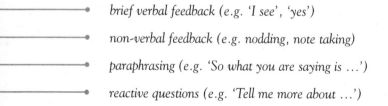

- *brief verbal feedback (e.g. 'I see', 'yes')*
- *non-verbal feedback (e.g. nodding, note taking)*
- *paraphrasing (e.g. 'So what you are saying is …')*
- *reactive questions (e.g. 'Tell me more about …')*

In addition, listen to what the customer does not say as well as what is said. For example, listen for hesitations and omissions, or words tinged with sarcasm or insincerity. In other words, aim to recognise not only the words but the true meaning behind them. Apparently it takes about three weeks of continuous effort to learn a new behaviour to the point where it becomes habitual. So why not resolve to spend the next three weeks learning to become an expert listener?

(137) Sell matching benefits

It's a well known fact that you don't sell product or service features, you sell the benefits to the customer that those features represent. Whereas the term 'features' refers to the hard facts that describe your company's products and services, a 'benefit' is what a product or service can do for the customer. This necessitates that you make explicit the link between a product or service feature and its benefit to the customer. An effective technique for doing this is to use the phrase 'which means that...' (or its equivalent, such as 'and what this means to you is...'), because it forces you to go on to explain how a particular feature benefits the customer. For example, the computer salesperson might say:

> *The speed of this printer is twice as fast as your existing system* ... (feature)
> *... which means that* ... (link)
> *you will cut printing times by 50 per cent* (benefit).

A useful exercise is to list all the features of your product or service and then to think through the benefit of each one to the customer. However, although benefit selling is a vital skill area, many salespeople fail to appreciate that successful selling is not about selling the same benefits to all customers all of the time. Rather, the key is to focus only on selling matching benefits, because the same product or service will almost always benefit different customers in different ways, depending on their individual circumstances. What makes your product or service superior to another is not the fact that it has more features, and consequently more benefits, but that it does more of what a particular customer wants it to do.

(138) Make yourself an indispensable component of your offer

Whatever else your competitors have to offer the customer, it is always well worth remembering that they don't have you! They don't have access to your experience, knowledge or expertise and, most of all, they don't have your commitment and enthusiasm to providing the best possible customer service. So ask yourself: 'What could I do to improve the value to the customer of my offer compared to my competitor's offer?' Better still, why not ask the customer? Showing your customers that you are prepared to 'go the extra mile' can be very compelling. Quite often people will be far more convinced by the depth of your conviction than the height of your logic. So the next time you are struggling to close a sale, don't forget to make yourself an indispensable component of your company's offer. It's a great way to differentiate yourself from the competition, win your customer's confidence, and tip the balance in your favour.

139 Look out for buying signals

When is the right time to ask that closing question? It's when our customers give us a buying signal. A buying signal is anything a customer says or does which suggests they're deciding to go ahead. Indeed, it is worth noting that when people talk about the need for good timing in selling, they are referring to the salesperson's ability to recognise and respond appropriately to a buying signal. Here are some classic examples to look out for:

- *Questions regarding terms, such as 'How much is it?'*

- *Positive body language, such as when the customer picks up the product to take a closer look.*

- *When you get their agreement on a series of key points.*

- *When you notice that they're talking past the sale; that is, talking as if they already own your product or service.*

- *When they offer you an additional argument to support your case.*

Always make sure you're fully tuned-in to watching and listening for buying signals, because every time you miss one you're throwing away an opportunity to close the sale. This is very easily done, especially when you become too preoccupied with trying to get your sales points across to the customer. Therefore, before you go into your next sales presentation, it is well worth the effort to prepare a list of all the buying signals you normally receive from your customers and decide on the best way to respond to each one. In compiling your list, note that some buying signals are stronger than others in that they indicate a greater degree of interest. For example, asking 'How much is it?' is usually a much stronger signal than picking up the product to take a closer look. Generally speaking, when you receive a weak buying signal, your best response is to ask a trial closing question (see idea 140). When you receive a stronger buying signal, however, this is the time to ask for the business outright with a direct closing question (see idea 141).

140 Ask plenty of trial closing questions

A trial close question is a conditional question such as an 'If ... then ...' or 'suppose ...' type of question, and the time to ask it is in response to a weak buying signal. Let's say, for example, the customer has expressed a tentative interest in some special finance terms. At this point, after a brief moment of silence you might say:

> *Jim, if we could do those terms for you, then would you place an order today?*

or

> *Let's suppose, just for a moment, that we could arrange that for you, Jim. Are you saying that you'd be prepared to go ahead on that basis?*

The key advantage of a trial closing question is that a negative response does not lock you out of the sale, because it is conditional upon something. If you get a positive response, however, all you have to do is satisfy the condition and the business is closed. In this way, trial closing questions avoid showdowns while still moving you closer to a sale. In short, they're dynamite! Use them liberally throughout your sales presentation as a means of 'testing out the temperature of the sale' whenever you receive a weak or subtle form of buying signal from the customer. You'll manufacture more closing situations and make more sales.

141 Master the direct close

In contrast to a trial closing question, a direct closing question is when you ask for the business outright, and the time to ask it is in response to a strong buying signal. If you've ever read any sales books, then you'll know there are literally dozens of different closing techniques from which to choose. Many of them concern me, however, because they seem to imply that tricking the customer into saying yes is what closing is all about.

Surely it should be a lot simpler than that! If you've received a strong buying signal, why not just go for it? There's really no substitute for the direct close. Just look the customer straight in the eye and, with a tone of confident expectation in your voice, ask for the business! Here are a couple of examples:

> **Example 1**
> Customer: 'How much is it?' (*buying signal*)
> Salesperson: 'It's $495. Would you like one?'
> **Example 2**
> Customer: 'It looks perfect.' (*buying signal*)
> Salesperson: 'Great! Can I write up your order?'

(142) Treat an objection as an opportunity

An objection is when the customer responds negatively in some way to your proposition. Whereas poor salespeople dread objections because they believe the customer is using them to block the sale, successful salespeople welcome them as requests for help and further information, and highlighting those issues of particular importance to the customer. In other words, they treat it as a buying signal. The key to handling objections, therefore, is to view them as an opportunity to dispel any areas of doubt in the customer's mind and to close the business.

Turning an objection into a closing opportunity is a three-step process. Assuming it is a genuine objection, the first step is to trial close on it. For example, you might say something like this:

> *Jim, if I could answer that point to your complete satisfaction, then would you be prepared to go ahead?*

If at this stage the customer agrees, then the business is closed, subject to the objection being handled to the customer's satisfaction. If, on the other hand, the customer responds negatively, then you must probe to find out what else is holding them back, and then trial close again.

The second step in handling the objection is to counter it. The means by which you counter an objection is in one of three ways:

> 1 *Drown it* by explaining how in their case the advantages outweigh the disadvantages.

2 Dilute it by explaining how, in practice, it would not really prove to be such a serious problem for them.

3 Disarm it by showing how it would not apply in their particular case.

Note that there is absolutely no reason whatsoever why you should not be able to anticipate virtually all the objections you are likely to encounter, and practise and rehearse your answers to perfection.

The third step of the process is to keep control. This means asking whether you have answered the objection to your customer's complete satisfaction. If the answer is no, then you have no option but to find out why and try once again to answer it to their complete satisfaction. If, on the other hand, the answer is yes, then providing you had wrapped a trial closing question around the objection when it was first raised, then the business is closed. All you have to do is take the order!

143 Overcome price objections by adding, subtracting, dividing and multiplying

There are two keys to successfully handling price objections. The first key is to accept responsibility for it. This means adopting the attitude that you obviously haven't yet sufficiently convinced the customer of the true value for money that your price represents. The second key is to go ahead and do the convincing. This can be done most effectively by using the four tools—adding, subtracting, dividing and multiplying—as follows:

+ *Add up every feature and benefit to justify and defend your price.* For example:
'Just so you know exactly what you'd be getting for your money, let's run through all the features and benefits again ...'

− *Subtract the features and benefits the customer wants but will not get by buying cheaper.* For example:
'Lets take a closer look at all the features you've said you wanted, but won't get by buying cheaper. You won't get ...'

÷ *Divide your price by the lifetime expectancy of your product— then 'reduce to the ridiculous' e.g. price per day.* For example:
'The extra $250 a year only works out to be about $5 a week— that's a dollar a day—about the price of your daily newspaper!'

> ✗ *Multiply the hidden costs of buying inferior quality products and services in the mind of the customer.* For example: 'Tell me, next time there's a breakdown emergency in your factory and you urgently need a service engineer, then what price is the peace of mind that comes with a reputation like ours?'

Be sure to anticipate all the price objections you're likely to encounter, and then use these four tools to prepare your responses in advance. Inevitably, in a competitive market, some price objections will relate directly to the customer's perception of the value of your offer versus those of your competitors. So in preparing your responses, make sure you are fully conversant with all the unique selling points of your company's proposition. Selling against the competition is all about selling the difference between what your price and what your competitor's price represents in terms of value to the customer.

(144) Use the 'try before you buy' close

In a face-to-face selling situation, it usually proves to be an irresistible offer to let your prospects 'try before they buy' and enjoy the benefits of your product during a free trial period. Providing your product lends itself to this idea, it's a great way to reduce sales resistance, and gives your product the chance to sell itself. The best thing about this idea, though, is that the more your prospect gets used to using your product, the more likely it is that they will want to keep it when you go back to sign them up. Make the buyer a proposition:

> *I'll tell you what, Jim, I'll leave it with you for a week and then if you like it you can pay for it, but if you don't, I'll take it away no questions asked. How's that?*

Make sure they feel under no obligation to keep the product, with nothing to sign. However, the more you can make it a fixture or fitting the better. For example, when sales representatives from a well known hand cleaner company call on motor mechanics, they attach their degreasing hand cleaner dispenser unit right above the workshop sink! Most importantly, time your return visit to coincide with the time when your prospect is likely to have taken psychological ownership. To continue our example, that's just as the mechanics are asking their boss: 'When are we going to get some more of this hand cleaner?'

Try the ATTACK formula

After a long and hard sales presentation, some customers will just thank you politely and say they'll be in touch after they have had time to think about it. Needless to say, under these circumstances, 'I want to think about it' is one of the most frustrating and difficult objections to overcome because, in a sense, the customer is not really objecting to the substance of your offer at all. Consequently, you have two basic choices. Depending on your reading of the situation you can either adopt a defensive stance; which means taking the customer at their word and booking a return visit, or you can decide to go on the offensive by using the ATTACK formula. Each letter of the acronym ATTACK stands for an action step in a series of steps that can help you turn this situation around into a sale. Notably, however, the ATTACK formula cannot compensate for a poor presentation. It simply enables you to draw upon a wide range of selling skills in a structured way, as a means of encouraging the customer to make a positive decision and not to procrastinate unnecessarily. The ATTACK sequence goes like this:

A = *Ask what areas of doubt still remain.* For example: 'I agree you should think about it, but in my experience this usually means people are unsure of certain points. May I ask what's on your mind …?'

T = *Transcribe each of the customer's points onto a master list.* For example: 'Okay, let's list them all out and see what we're talking about here …' (get them all).

T = *Trial close before attempting to answer the points on the list.* For example: 'So if I could deal with all these points to your complete satisfaction, then would you place an order?'

A = *Answer each point to the customer's satisfaction, then cross it off the list.* For example: 'I'm glad we've cleared that one up, so can I cross it off the list now?'

C = *Close the sale by asking an alternative closing question.* For example: 'Great, that's everything covered, so would you like it delivered next Monday, or would this Friday suit you better?'

K = *Keep quiet and don't deflect the customer's mind away from making a decision!*

Sell add-ons whenever you can

Providing your company offers a range of products and services, then one of the best ways of increasing the size of your average sale is to take the opportunity to sell add-ons whenever you can. This can be achieved by asking your customer an appropriate question at the appropriate time, in exactly the same way as McDonald's staff always ask '… and would you like fries with that?', or the menswear salesperson asks '… and would you like a tie to go with your new shirt?' Of course, even though the vast majority of customers will decline this invitation, think how many extra portions of fries and new ties are sold every day as a direct result of this question—sales that otherwise would have been missed!

As you can see, when selling add-ons, the trick is simply to get into the habit of always asking a question that gives your customer the opportunity to buy something else that can be used in conjunction with their initial purchase. Most importantly however, don't ask this question in such a way that your customer will feel over pressured. Simply ask it in a businesslike way that comes across as a natural part of the high standard of service that you offer to customers.

10

CHAPTER

IDEAS FOR NEGOTIATING
MORE PROFITABLE SALES
FACE-TO-FACE

Sales negotiation is an important aspect of face-to-face selling that takes place whenever the buyer becomes committed in principle to making a purchase, but then starts to argue over terms and conditions. It takes the form of a 'trading and exchange' process for the specific purpose of identifying a mutually acceptable price–package combination.

Owner–managers of successful small businesses know how important it is to be fully prepared for the negotiation phase of the sale—not least because most professional buyers are highly trained negotiators armed with a whole range of tactics for squeezing the lowest possible price out of ill-prepared salespeople.

Successful sales
negotiating is a game
of tactics and
countermeasures: learn
to play and play to win.

Establish a climate of agreement

As you move into the negotiation phase of the sale, if you are genuine about aiming for a win–win outcome with a view to building long-term customer relationships, then why not tell your buyer just that? For example, you could say:

> Jim, I'd like you to know my philosophy is always to find a good deal for both parties...I'd like to think that we can both come out as winners today and build a solid base for future business between us. Fair enough?

Make it clear that you are open to any suggestions that will make the deal more acceptable and do your utmost to encourage your buyer to think likewise. It's a great way of building trust and signalling that you favour a cooperative and creative negotiation style rather than an aggressive, competitive approach.

Know your bottom line

It's often said that negotiating skills make the difference between making a sale and making a profitable sale. However, this assertion is based on the assumption that the salesperson knows the difference between the two— and I'm not sure that's always the case. What I'm saying is that, whereas everyone knows what their ideal outcome or 'top line' looks like, that's the easy part! The difficult bit is knowing where to draw the 'bottom line'—the one that separates an acceptable and profitable deal from one that isn't.

The point is, in order to negotiate, you have to have something to negotiate with and that something is the difference between your top and bottom lines. Of course, you always have to be prepared to compromise on your top line, but equally, you have to know when to walk away from a deal that's not going to be worth your while. So always make sure you know your bottom line because you can't negotiate without one!

Identify all the non-price variables important to your buyer

Effective sales negotiating is not about haggling over price. On the contrary, it is about identifying all the non-price variables important to the buyer and taking the view that the price is just a part (albeit an important part) of the whole package. To put it another way, it is to trade off your price against the other elements of the deal. The aim is to find a price–package combination that maximises value to the buyer as well as profit to you as the supplier, so your key task is to find out which elements of the deal are negotiable to the benefit of both parties. In finding out what else is important to your buyer, other than price, there are seven main areas upon which to focus your efforts when questioning your buyer about their requirements. I call these areas the seven Ss because they all start with the letter 'S':

1 Specifications of product. This area relates to the level of product quality required, or the range of features (and consequent benefits) the customer wants included. In the business-to-business environment, such specification requirements can vary greatly.

2 Service level. This area relates to services such as installation, maintenance, product training or inventory control. An extremely high level of service provision may well be needed in some cases, whereas in others (for example where there is already an in-house capability) there may be no need whatsoever.

3 Scope of warranty/guarantee. This area relates to the level of requirement for various forms of 'insurance cover' surrounding the purchase decision. This includes both the type of cover required and the length of time for which the cover is required.

4 Span of contract. This area relates to the buyer's need to build a partnership with suppliers in order to ensure continuity of supply over time. Under these circumstances, the buyer and seller must agree to the terms of a contract which specifies the precise nature of their business relationship and commitments over a set period.

5 Size of order. This area relates to the extent to which the buyer wishes to take advantage of what may be described as 'scale economies' in the purchase decision. This occurs when larger orders can be translated into lower prices. The main consideration here, therefore, is the volume of goods that is, or could be, required by the buyer over the foreseeable future.

6 Special payment terms. This area relates to the buyer's preference for a method of payment other than cash. For example, they may wish to take advantage of special finance or credit facilities (such as a leasing or hire purchase agreement), or a more unconventional approach such as a contra-deal, an allowance of some kind or a part-exchange deal.

7 Speed of delivery. This area relates to the degree of urgency attached to the buyer's requirements at the time of purchase.

150 Explore the personal interests of the buyer

Make a note of the following story:

> Once upon a time there were two sisters, and one day they both went to get an orange from the fruit bowl. Unfortunately though, there was only one orange left. So they started to squabble, and after about 10 minutes they decided the only way to resolve the argument was to cut it straight down the middle and take half each. But guess what happened next—one sister went into her room, ate the fruit and threw away the peel while the other went into the kitchen, threw away the fruit and used the peel to bake a cake!

Well it's a great story isn't it, and the moral is that it's well worth exploring the personal interests of the buyers. Always go beyond just finding out what buyers want and try and find out *why* they want it. For example, a little investigation might reveal that your buyer is interested in such things as being seen to be 'politically correct', minimising their workload or avoiding risks at all costs; and that's the kind of information you can use to your advantage.

151 In making your opening proposal, aim high

In making your opening proposal, take each item of your buyer's shopping list and say what you're prepared to do for them as part of a new package deal. Always take the time to explain the benefits and, if possible, try and introduce a new variable into your package. Most importantly though, make sure that your new package doesn't represent a 'price compromise', but simply a reshuffling of all the variables that make up the deal.

Those salespeople who start giving in to the buyer's demands too early usually end up coming away with a far worse deal than those who hold firm. The successful sales negotiator gives away very little, if anything, when making an opening proposal. Generally speaking, the lower you aim, the less you'll get, whereas the higher you aim, the more you'll get.

152 Trade concessions—don't give them away!

One of the key principles of sales negotiating is never to give away a concession without getting something back in return. Sales negotiating is about trading concessions, not giving them away! The idea that throwing in this or that free of charge will somehow soften up a professional buyer and enable you to 'buy' an agreement to a particular price–package is a myth. In buyer–seller relationships, generosity is not contagious. A professional buyer will just take any concession on offer, say 'thanks very much', and then keep on pushing for more until they have taken you for all you have got! That's why the most powerful question in the professional sales negotiator's toolkit is the conditional 'if … then' style, because it enables you to explore trading opportunities without letting go of your opening position. Here it is:

If we do that for you, then what can you do for us in return?

For example, if the buyer hints that your opening proposal might be acceptable for an extra 5 per cent discount, then just treat it as a trading opportunity. In these circumstances, asking an 'if…then' style question should be a reflex response.

153 Never say yes to the buyer's first proposal

Imagine the scene. You advertise your car for $2000 and within an hour a potential buyer turns up to inspect it. After five minutes of looking over the car, they offer to buy it for $1800 cash on the spot. You accept, take the money, hand over the car keys and watch the buyer drive away in the car. Now, ask yourself this: how would you feel about that deal? At first you'd probably feel quite happy, but you'd inevitably end up wondering what would have happened if you'd held out for $2000—after all, the buyer did seem keen to buy! Then ask yourself this: how would the buyer be feeling? Well, most likely, just like you, the buyer would probably have felt quite happy at first, but pretty soon would almost certainly have been wishing they had only offered you $1600—after all, you had seemed so keen to sell!

Of course, this is an oversimplified example, but the point is that this was a bad deal because neither party felt satisfied they had got the best possible deal for themselves. That's why it is important never to let your buyers come away from a deal wondering if they could have done better. Even when you actually like the sound of the buyer's opening proposal (it can happen!), do not accept it immediately. Instead, make the buyer work harder, because the harder your buyer works for a deal, the happier they will be with it afterwards. One of the golden rules of sales negotiating is never to say yes to the buyer's first proposal.

 ## Look out for the 'If I buy this, and this ...' tactic

In your role as the buyer, I'm sure you'll have used this tactic at one time or another. For example, in a clothes shop you've probably asked the shopkeeper: 'If I buy the suit and the shirt, will you throw in the tie?' or words to that effect. How should a salesperson counter this tactic? Well assuming the scale of the buyer's request is relativity minor, then your first response should be to view it as a positive sign, because when a buyer resorts to this kind of terminology, it usually means you're getting close to a deal. However, never give in to this kind of request and always treat it seriously by using your calculator and visibly taking your time to work out just how much discount their request actually represents. For example, let's say you're the salesperson in the clothes shop, and the price of the tie is $80. Then you might say:

> I sell five of these suits a week, Jim, so what you're suggesting is that I give away $400 a week—that's $20 800 a year!

If necessary, write it down and let the buyer see the cost implications of their request and then keep quiet. If this fails to put the buyer off, then say you're quite happy to throw in whatever it is, providing they do something for you in return, such as placing a regular order. Remember, never give away a concession without getting something back in return.

 ## Exercise your expertise power

As an experienced professional salesperson, the chances are you know more about your industry, your market, your competitors and your products and services than just about any other person alive—and don't forget, that includes your buyer! The fact is, you are an expert, and let's make no mistake about it, in a negotiation that expertise is a powerful persuasive force. This is because the more the buyer sees you in the role of expert, the more likely they are to defer to you in helping to shape the deal to their best advantage. In short, people trust an expert. So how can you make the most of your expertise power? Well obviously, you need to present yourself as an expert—and that means, looking, acting and talking like one. More importantly, however, it means making your opinions, knowledge and experience an invaluable part of the deal-making process.

156 Conceal your emotions

Imagine you are in a camera crew filming a group of professional poker players around a table in a plush hotel room. There's a hushed silence and a huge pile of money in the middle of the table. It is all to play for, and there are only two players left in the game. Each one is studying their cards closely as they decide on their next move. Now, imagine you zoom in for a close-up of their body language and facial expressions—what do you think they would look like? Of course, the chances are that neither player would be giving anything away, and the best description of their expressions would be 'deadpan'.

Now imagine a professional buyer and a highly experienced salesperson at the negotiating table. They are at a critical stage of the negotiation process and each one is anxious to cut the best possible deal. How would their facial expressions be likely to compare with those of the poker players?

Obviously there is quite a strong comparison to be drawn between these two scenarios because in both cases, to a large extent, the outcome depends on an ability to conceal your emotions. Make no mistake about it, emotions are like words. The more you express them in the form of your body language or facial expressions, the more information you are giving away. Any obvious expressions of relief, elation, panic or whatever simply provide the buyer with valuable clues about your position, and this kind of information will always be used against you. When negotiating, be like a poker player and try to keep a straight face, no matter what.

157 Harness print power

The fact that something is printed tends to enhance its believability. It has a kind of built-in authority that the spoken word or handwritten materials just cannot match.

You will probably have noticed how professional buyers are particularly adept at using pre-printed materials to their advantage. During the course of a sales negotiation they will routinely produce all sorts of printed matter to underline their authority, justify their position and undermine the aspiration levels of the salesperson. These include quotes from other suppliers, price breakdowns, budget statements and business plans, to name but a few. But don't be intimidated! In fact, make sure you are suitably armed with such printed matter yourself, and at least in equal measure. For example, price lists can help to 'legitimise' your prices. Charts, graphs, letters from satisfied customers, copies of journal articles and the like can also be used to help substantiate your selling points. In addition, use as many types of 'fill in the blanks' paperwork as you can as an aid to the negotiation process. The more you can refer to a whole range of pre-printed material during the course of a sale, the more you will come across as credible, believable and professional in the eyes of the buyer.

Keep price breakdown information to yourself

A friend who collects vases once explained how she used the classic 'price breakdown' buying tactic to acquire a magnificent hand-painted vase for a rock bottom price. Here's her story:

> One Sunday afternoon, she was out for a walk exploring some city side streets when she came across an arts and crafts store she hadn't seen before. Peering in through the window she spotted a glorious pair of huge ceramic vases which, apart from the hand-painted designs, were identical. Finding herself unable to resist the temptation to buy, she went straight inside and proceeded to push the shopkeeper to give her his best price for the two vases. In the end, his very best price was $1000. She then pretended to be interested in her least favourite of the two vases and asked him to give her his very best price for just that one vase—$600 came the reply. 'Oh well', said my friend, in a mock disappointed tone of voice, 'in that case, I'll take the other one for $400!'

Well it's a neat little story that does make a point rather well, don't you think? The point being that, in a sales negotiating situation, a professional buyer will ALWAYS push you for price breakdown information, and the more you give them, the more they'll use it against you! That's why you should always keep price breakdown information to yourself.

159 Use the 'continuous-yes' summary close

Arguably, the most useful closing method in sales negotiation is the 'continuous-yes' summary close. Indeed, the longer the negotiation takes, and the more difficult it becomes, the greater the potential effectiveness of this close because (as you will see in the example below) it relies on a strong build-up. The continuous-yes close is particularly useful when you reach a point in the negotiation where your latest proposal is very close to being acceptable, and it's worth pushing for a decision.

In using the continuous-yes close, the aim is to gain the buyer's agreement to each of the benefits on offer during the course of your summary before respectfully asking for their agreement to go ahead. For example:

Salesperson: *Jim, let me quickly run through what you'd be getting with this deal. You said you wanted the turbo system so that you could be sure to achieve your production targets, is that right?*
Buyer: *Yes, that's right.*
Salesperson: *Okay, and you also said you wanted the peace of mind that comes with our five-star service scheme, didn't you?*
Buyer: *Yes, I did.* (and so on)

By stacking these 'say yes' questions one after another, the buyer is encouraged to recognise and appreciate fully all the positive aspects of the deal that's on the table. This makes it more likely that they will continue to say yes when you conclude your summary by asking for an agreement!

160 Always do some paperwork

As soon as you you've reached a final agreement, depending on the complexity of the deal, you may or may not be in a position to do the formal paperwork. If you can, so much the better. Get it over and done with. If you can't, however (for whatever reason), then always make a point of getting a signature anyway, just to be on the safe side. In case you have any doubts about the wisdom of this approach, remember the old adage:

A verbal contract isn't worth the paper it's written on!

Here's how to do it. As soon as you have struck the deal, take the time to summarise your understanding of the terms of your agreement and jot down the key points on a separate piece of paper. Then suggest that before you leave it might be a good idea to photocopy it and initial each other's copy, just for the record, prior to the completion of the formal paperwork. The beauty of this idea is that if the buyer says yes, you can be sure you have absolute clarity regarding the terms of the deal. If, on the other hand, the buyer hesitates in some way, then you have an ideal opportunity to iron out any areas of misunderstanding before you leave.

161 Congratulate the buyer!

Having successfully concluded a negotiated sale, it is very important to make a special point of congratulating your buyer on making their purchase and on the way they handled the negotiation. What's more, when doing so, be sure to look your buyer straight in the eye and to offer a firm handshake (being especially careful, of course, not to show even the slightest hint of triumph!). No doubt you will have both worked hard to reach a final agreement, so you might as well celebrate it. Always leave your buyers feeling good about themselves and their purchases.

162 Leave the door open whenever there's an impasse

It's a fact of business life that there are always going to be those odd occasions when, for whatever reason, you just cannot persuade the buyer to go that last yard and a mutually acceptable deal cannot be struck. However, just because you cannot strike a deal now, does not necessarily mean you cannot strike one later. So whenever there is an impasse, it makes sense to leave the door open and give yourself one last chance of getting the business at a later date. Tell the buyer that, since you have both put so much time and effort into the negotiation, you would like to arrange to meet up again in a few days to see if either one of you can come up with any new ideas in the meantime. That way, you will at least be walking away with all your options fully intact, rather than closing the door on a deal unnecessarily. Book the date and time of your next meeting before you leave.

IDEAS FOR BUILDING STRONGER CUSTOMER RELATIONSHIPS

The term 'customer relationships' refers to the extent to which there is a feeling of relatedness and rapport between a company and its customers.

Owner–managers of successful small businesses attach a high priority to making sure their customers keep coming back. They know that selling to an existing customer is far more cost-effective than chasing a potential new one. So a lot of time and effort is devoted to keeping in touch with customers, building relationships and, making sure they are always completely satisfied.

Many businesspeople see the sale as the end of the selling process, whereas most customers see it as just the beginning of a relationship.

Say thanks with thank you slips

Thank you. Said with genuine sincerity, these words are among the most powerful in any businessperson's toolkit. It is important to appreciate, however, that I'm not simply referring to saying 'thank you' at the point of sale. In fact, I believe it's when you say it at a different point in time, *a day or two after the sale*, that it becomes truly memorable and meaningful to customers. That's why 'thank you' slips are the perfect complement to the more traditional 'with compliments' slips. They're ideal for all those occasions when we've taken something rather than given something, such as when we've received confirmation of an order, a cheque or a signed contract! They're very personal and show that you and your company are genuinely appreciative of receiving a customer's business. Here's how to go about making the most of them.

Use the same format as a 'with compliments' slip and just change the words to 'thank you'. To add a little razzamatazz, have the words printed in a number of different languages such as *merci, danke, grazie* and so on, just as long as there's plenty of empty space left for you to write in a personal message.

From now on, make sure that every new sale is followed up by a personal and professional thanks by sending one of these. Needless to say, as well as thanking customers for buying, there are plenty of other occasions when sending a 'thank you' slip would be appropriate. For example, when someone has given you a referral or passed on a piece of useful information, or when a complaint has been successfully resolved.

 ## Present commemorative plaques

When your company reaches a landmark, such as 10 years in business, or when your company's sales figures finally hit the one million dollar mark, why not celebrate the event by giving your best and most faithful customers a plaque to commemorate the occasion? It's an effective way to build customer loyalty and cement longstanding relationships, while at the same time creating a mutually beneficial publicity opportunity. Here's how to do it.

Design a commemorative plaque and have copies made for each of your top 20 customers. Use a specialist retailer who can help you decide on the most appropriate and cost-effective design and style for your kind of business. Have the plaques inscribed with a personal thank you together with a 'without your help we couldn't have done it' message. Invite the press along to a group presentation and ensure that all your customers get due recognition. This will cement your business relationship with them and hopefully lay the foundation for another 10 years of doing business together!

It always surprises me just how much people enjoy receiving a small token of appreciation. An elderly managing director I know who was presented with one such little plaque by one of his suppliers over 30 years ago still gives it pride of place on his office mantelpiece. Imagine that— the memory of a simple thank you lovingly cared for and cherished (and no doubt commented upon) for over 30 years!

165 Launch a sow and grow competition

This is a fun idea I learned from an insurance company. For many years their salespeople held a competition among corporate customers to see who could grow the best crop of miniature tomatoes from the seedlings they supplied at the beginning of the year. It was a fun idea that didn't require any effort on the part of the customer and yet it succeeded in providing their salespeople with a ready-made talking point throughout the year, ensuring the door was always open for them to go back repeatedly to talk business. What's more, it's a great way to help develop customer relationships. Here's how to do it.

At the beginning of the year, visit selected customers and present them with a seedling, explaining that there will be a prize for the best crop of tomatoes at the end of the year. Supply the seedling in a large pot with your company name and logo on it and arrange to leave it in a place where it is sure to be noticed, such as in a stairway, corridor or tea room.

Visit on a regular basis to monitor the growth of your plant and tend to it if necessary, and while you're there take the opportunity to talk business. Conclude the competition by presenting lots of fun prizes and, if you'll pardon the pun, you'll be sowing the seeds of long-lasting customer relationships.

166 Pay unexpected attentions

Giving 'unexpected attentions' is the simple idea of delighting your customers by sending them a little something from time to time— something that's totally unexpected. It works well as a relationship builder because whenever anyone goes out of their way to do something for someone else, and especially when they do it without having been asked, it never goes unnoticed. To put it another way, in an increasingly impersonal world, little things mean a lot to people.

The key to this idea is to seize any opportunity you can to pass on useful information to your customers. For example, it might be a copy of an interesting magazine article, information about a new invention or technological breakthrough in your industry, details of a good business book you've come across, a promotional idea, or even just a humorous anecdote or cartoon that relates to them or their business in some way. It is usually necessary to photocopy or re-package the material so it's smartly presented before posting it out to customers together with a 'with compliments' slip that simply says 'Thought you might like a copy of this', preferably handwritten and signed by you. Repeat the gesture whenever anything interesting catches your eye. Best of all, if you sell to businesses, make sure you pass on any sales leads whenever you get the chance. Your customers will love you for it!

167 Give away functional freebies

'Freebies' are those promotional giveaways that most companies shower upon their customers and prospects to maintain goodwill and name awareness. However, the golden rule to remember when giving away freebies is this:

Freebies work harder for you when they work harder for your customers.

What this means is that you should avoid giving away ordinary freebies such as pens or key rings. Instead, make sure your freebies serve a genuinely valuable purpose—and one that's related in some way to your product or service. What's more, make sure they are of a reasonable quality, or the reputation that you'll gain will be for giving away junk! The aim is for customers to look forward to receiving a freebie from your company because they know it will be a good one.

Make your choice of freebie by asking yourself what items would naturally complement the use of your products and services. In other words, choose freebies which are sure to be noticed because they'll be constantly in use. For example, the chemical company that gives away safety goggles, the computer company that gives away mouse mats, or the management training company that gives away desk plaques inscribed with a useful motto.

Ensure your freebies carry your company name and logo together with a short sales message. Give them away selectively and with no strings attached. That way they are seen purely as a goodwill gesture and will serve to strengthen your relationships with customers.

168 Develop a service vision

The most successful small business operators are those with vision. Read the following example and you'll see exactly what I mean:

> I used to go to a certain hairdressing salon on a regular basis. Even though it was a bit more expensive than most, I liked going there because the routine would always be the same. As soon as I'd set foot in the place, I'd be given a cheery first-name greeting. Within an instant, someone would be taking my coat and leading me over to a luxurious seating area with plenty of glossy magazines to read. Then they would bring me a cup of fresh coffee together with my favourite Danish pastry. A few minutes later my stylist, Jay (also the owner of the salon), would welcome me and take me through to a private room for a personal consultation. Referring back to my client card, she'd proceed to ask me a series of questions about my requirements, recommend a style, and prescribe some hair care products if needed. Next I'd have my hair washed and be given an invigorating neck massage. Having been escorted to my stylist's chair and offered another cup of coffee, I'd then enjoy an interesting chat (guaranteed to be interesting because it was usually all about me!) with Jay as she cut my hair. Occasionally other members of staff would interrupt to say hi and exchange a few words, all of which made me feel like I was part of the family. Finally, Jay would always check that I was completely happy with my haircut before selling me whatever hair care products I needed and taking my money. Then she'd book me in for my next appointment, walk me to the door and wish me a fond farewell.

When I complimented Jay one day on what a great business she ran, I was fascinated to learn that not one aspect of the service I or anyone else received was ever left to chance. Although on the surface the business appeared to operate in a casual and spontaneous manner, this was not the case. Jay explained to me that the key to success in her business was to provide such a high standard of friendly personal service that her customers would develop a sense of loyalty and want to keep on coming back. This meant she had worked hard with her staff during training sessions to develop a 'service vision' for the salon. As a result, everyone knew how to deal with customers according to the same vision which, as

Jay explained it, was a sort of 'video film' which each member of her staff could easily imagine, in great detail, on the screen of their mind. As Jay was quick to point out, however, the most powerful part of their vision was not so much to do with the step-by-step process of their service provision as it was to do with the creation of the right kind of friendly, relaxed, welcoming and happy atmosphere that was so crucial to the success of their business. What a great idea! If you operate in a similar service environment, start working with your staff to develop an appropriate service vision for your business.

169 Stay in touch

Like most people, you probably have friends dotted around the world that you haven't seen in ages. Yet you still think of them as friends because year in, year out, they never forget to send you a birthday or Christmas card—right? Well, it's a simple enough idea, which is why it never ceases to amaze me that so few businesspeople see fit to stay in touch with their customers in this way. After all, it's a relatively quick and inexpensive method of creating and maintaining a feeling of friendliness between you and your customer. Above all, it's a way of adding the personal touch to your business communications.

There are plenty of special occasions, other than birthdays and Christmas, when you could take the opportunity to stay in touch with your customers by sending a card. Those occasions that apply particularly well to a business selling direct to individual members of the public include New Year (instead of Christmas perhaps?), Easter, Valentine's Day, Mother's Day, Father's Day, marriages and wedding anniversaries, or any other uniquely personal special occasion. Although not all of the above may be equally as applicable to businesses that sell to other businesses, of particular importance would be to send a card when someone is promoted, relocated to another office or factory, wins an industry award, launches a new product or becomes professionally qualified.

In order to make the most of this idea, you could keep a large calendar on the wall which highlights any special dates or occasions not to be missed, especially those that relate to specific customers for a specific reason. An even easier way, however, is to use a computer. By keeping customer information files on computer, you can easily create and print out your mailings at the touch of a button on a weekly or even daily basis.

Encourage customer complaints

There are two main reasons why you should make it easy for your customers to complain. First, you can eliminate a lot of bad publicity. Research shows that customers who suffer in silence will, on average, tell about 10 other people just how poor they think your product or service is before switching to another supplier. Second, if you can successfully resolve a customer's complaint to their total satisfaction, then more often than not you'll have succeeded in creating a customer who is more loyal than one who was adequately satisfied in the first place. The fact is, when you resolve a customer's problem promptly and with good grace, they will typically experience a sense of obligation to buy from you again and to tell other people about you.

Always resist the temptation to see customer complaints as a problem. Instead, look at them as an opportunity and encourage them. This is very simply done. All you have to do is to tell customers that, as part of your company's commitment to satisfying its customers, you'd welcome the opportunity to sort out any problems they may have, no matter how small. Better still, put it in the form of a personal promise or pledge and feature it in your guarantees or service backup policies as an integral part of your advertising. This kind of approach is reassuring for existing customers and works especially well as an extra reason for new customers to buy from you rather than from your competitors.

Next, you'll need to develop a complaints-handling procedure so that your staff know exactly what to do when a complaint is received. This means sitting down with them to decide on what kind of procedure will work best. You may find it useful to adopt and adapt the following nine-stage model. When I was the marketing director of a small computer company, this was the procedure we used for handling any customer complaints received by telephone:

1 Identify yourself.

2 Ask for the customer's name and telephone number.

3 Put yourself on their side—agree that the problem exists.

4 Say 'Let's see what I can do …'.

5 Listen and make notes.

6 Repeat the key points and check the facts.

7 Admit any mistakes and apologise for them.

8 Say what you can do to resolve the problem.

9 Follow through on your promises.

One last point. If necessary, it's always worth doing a little extra to keep a customer happy. For example, after a problem has been sorted out you could write a letter of apology (if the fault was yours) or a letter expressing your regret at their misfortune (if the fault was theirs). You might even see fit to send them a small gift. Always make the most of an opportunity to rebuild and strengthen your relationship with a customer.

171 Create a privileged customer group

Assuming you sell products or services that are re-purchased on a regular basis, by creating a privileged customer group you can make your best customers feel special. Offering them preferential terms and conditions which are only available to members helps develop customer loyalty and creates a highly receptive group of customers to whom you can direct future offers.

Select your privileged customer group by using the 80/20 rule. In other words, analyse your customer base and identify which are your best customers—the 20 per cent of your customers who bring in 80 per cent of your profits. Give your privileged customer group an exclusive sounding title such as 'The VIP Club' or something similar, and design a special gold card which can even be personalised to each member. Also, be sure to restrict the term of membership so that the card doesn't apply indefinitely.

Next, send a letter inviting selected customers to join your privileged customer group for a nominal fee of say $10, making sure to spell out the benefits of membership such as improved credit terms, extra discounts, preferential service, previews to special offers or some other special privileges. Note that a small membership fee is important because people always value something more when they have to pay for it. Then mail a steady flow of offers to your newly created client bank, encouraging them to benefit from membership by spending more.

172 Run a closed door sale

A 'closed door sale' is a promotional method that's ideal for retailers, or indeed any company which holds stock or finished product at their place of business. A closed door sale is exactly as the words imply. It's when you run an after hours, invitation-only sale, exclusively for your current customers and perhaps some of their friends or associates. With this idea you'll get an instant injection of cash, the immediate removal of aged or surplus stocks, and plenty of extra-satisfied customers.

The key to running a successful closed door sale is the letter of invitation you send out to customers. In your letter, it's important to create a sense of exclusivity that makes your customers feel special about having been invited. Insist that they respond to the invitation, and tempt them with the promise of at least one unbelievable offer that's just too good to miss. Run your closed door sale mid-week in the early evening, and be sure to make everyone feel welcome.

173 Invest in a welcoming board

I must admit, I really enjoy the feeling of walking into the reception area of a plush hotel. Everything is so immaculate and welcoming, and there's such an air of confidence and efficiency about the place. In particular, out of sheer curiosity I always look out for one of those easel-style welcoming boards that tells guests all about the day's activities. In fact, when you come to think of it, hotels are extremely good at creating exactly the kind of ambience that we should be striving to create in the reception areas of our own businesses. That is why I am convinced that every company should invest in a visitors' welcoming board for their reception area. It creates a strong first impression, makes your customers feel important and projects a highly professional company image. Best of all, it is a relatively inexpensive way to create a 'big company feel' in a small company's offices.

Having chosen an appropriate size and style of welcoming board, display it prominently so it's the first thing visitors see when they walk into your reception area. Most importantly, give it a big title, making sure to include your company name and your business slogan, such as:

Welcome to the Hamilton Oil Drum Company
'Our drums take some beating.'

Maximise impact by simply listing your visitor's name, their title and the name of their company. The only thing that people like more than the sound of their own name is the sight of it!

Be accessible 24/7

I'm sure you don't need reminding that the business world is becoming increasingly competitive. To put it another way, it's a buyer's market out there and that's the way it's going to be for a very long time. As a result, customers are demanding and receiving a level of personal service that perhaps only a decade or so ago would have been unthinkable. Long gone are the days when businesspeople could afford the luxury of 24-hour customer response times. These days we have to respond a lot more quickly than that or we'll soon lose out to the competition. That's why I believe every businessperson should seriously consider being accessible to customers 24 hours a day, seven days a week.

Before you fall off your chair in shock, let me explain what I mean by being 'accessible'. I'm not suggesting that we should be providing immediate service. Clearly for most businesses that would be both ridiculous and unnecessary (although not for all companies). What I'm saying is that, in order to compete these days, we should at least be able to be contacted around the clock. Let's face it, modern technology facilitates it, customers expect it, and the competition is offering it.

If you're not already doing so, why not give customers your mobile telephone number and tell them they can call you any time? Ideally, give them the full range of alternatives, including your after-hours telephone number, an email address and a fax number, and promote your unconditional accessibility as being 'all part of the service' on your business cards, promotional literature and other documentation. The beauty of this approach is that the smaller your business is, the more impressed and reassured your customers will be with your level of personal commitment to serving them.

Launch a frequent buyer program

A useful motto for any company selling products that are re-purchased on a regular basis might go like this:

We aim to sell products that don't come back to customers who do!

This motto is one of my favourites because it clearly communicates the need to create satisfied customers and then to keep them coming back to buy from you again and again. So, assuming you've already created a number of satisfied customers, then some kind of frequent buyer program could be just what you need to help keep your customers coming back.

My local coffee bar provides a good example of how to run a simple, yet highly effective type of frequent buyer program. When I go for a coffee I'm handed a small card containing seven coffee cup symbols underneath the name, address and telephone number of the coffee bar. The fourth and seventh coffee cups are over-printed in red ink with the word FREE in block capital letters. From then on, every time I go back for another coffee all I have to do is produce the card so the next cup in the sequence can be stamped, and I'm one cup closer to a free cappuccino. As you can see, the basic idea of any frequent buyer program is to offer your customers some kind of incentive to keep on buying from you.

In planning an appropriate frequent buyer program, the most important consideration is to decide precisely what sort of program to use and exactly how it will work. There are plenty of different examples around from which to choose (such as the 'frequent flyer' programs). However, be sure to think carefully before making your choice. Many programs are really only feasible for large companies because they require very sophisticated record keeping. The last thing you want is to launch a complicated program that could easily go wrong or backfire in some way. You could easily end up losing more customers than you keep!

Generally speaking, the easier a program is to understand and to operate, the better. A good tip is to always talk over your plans with a few customers before going ahead, to make sure it's likely to be of interest. What's more, always time-fuse your new frequent buyer program by making it clear to customers that it applies over a limited time period. That way, when it is over, you can evaluate its effectiveness and, if necessary, make any improvements or modifications before running it again.

176 Follow up everything with a telephone call

Take every opportunity you can to get personal. This can be as easy as making a telephone call. Here's an example:

> I'll never forget having one of my wisdom teeth taken out. It was only my second appointment with my new dentist, Dr Leatham. He had seen me a couple of weeks previously and told me that it was time to have the troublesome tooth extracted. However, the good news was that he thought I wouldn't have to go into hospital, and that he would be able to do it relatively quickly 'in the chair'.

When the fateful time arrived, I was somewhat heartened to learn that I was Dr Leatham's last appointment for the day. My appointment was at 5 p.m. so I figured that meant I'd only be in the chair for about half an hour at the most. Little did I know! An hour later I was still in the chair, and Dr Leatham was still pulling away at that darn tooth! I can't describe the pain, it was so bad. When it eventually came out, the attending nurse burst into applause and I could see the relief written all over Dr Leatham's face! He readily admitted that he'd made a mistake by suggesting he do it himself. Apparently, I should have been in hospital. As you can imagine, I was glad to get home that evening and went straight to bed armed with a glass of water and a handful of painkillers. All the same, against my better judgement I decided to go to work the following morning. Just as I was on my way out of the house, the telephone rang. To my astonishment, it was Dr Leatham ringing to see how I was.

Now all this happened a long time ago, and although the memory of the pain I endured has faded, I can still remember that telephone call and the effect it had on me as if it were yesterday. Frankly, I'm still amazed to think he bothered to make that call, and at the time I was so impressed that I instantly forgave him for not referring me on to a hospital in the first place, as he should have done. Despite my discomfort, I can remember singing his praises to everyone I met, and needless to say, I was a regular customer at Dr Leatham's dental clinic for a very long time.

Let's analyse that telephone call. How much did it cost? A few cents. How long did it take? Two minutes. Yet what was the effect on the customer? Priceless! Surely there's a lesson to be learned here. If we want to build long-lasting relationships with our customers, then there's no substitute for doing the simple things, like following up any service encounter with a telephone call to show our customers that we care. Especially when it's done by you, as the owner–manager of the business, the positive effects on the customer are always going to extend well beyond the time and money costs.

177 Start a mini-newsletter

A newsletter that goes out to customers on a six-monthly or quarterly basis can be an effective way of maintaining a high profile with your customers, cementing their allegiance and providing them with a potentially valuable additional service. Most importantly, by inviting contributions from your customers, you can actually get customers feeling as though it's their newsletter, not yours.

A good newsletter needn't cost a fortune to produce. The key is to put the emphasis on good content rather than worrying too much about its appearance. Above all, keep the layout and design simple. The most important thing is that it's easy to read and chatty. In fact, sometimes just an extended letter format can work well. Whatever style you choose, however, don't make it too long. Two sheets of A4 paper (perhaps folded into an A5 booklet) is usually about right, and it's always a good idea to get it pre-punched with holes so it will fit neatly into a ring binder. That way you'll be encouraging people to keep them, especially if each issue is numbered.

A simple format for a newsletter is as follows. Divide the contents of your newsletter into three main parts. In the first part, put the spotlight on your customers by inviting contributions from them and giving them a forum to tell everyone about themselves. Alternatively, simply print the transcripts of an interview with one of your best customers. In the second part, put the spotlight on your industry and encourage the exchange of facts and figures, tips and advice, or any other useful information, such as the details of any forthcoming industry exhibitions or seminars that may be of interest to your customers. A good tip is to invite contributions from other non-competing suppliers serving your marketplace. In the third part, include a regular feature on yourselves—providing customers with a brief personal message from your managing director and any news relating to your people, products and services, together with an up-to-date sales information service.

Once you're up and running with your newsletter, invite customer feedback to see what they think of it and how it could be improved. The more you involve your customers in all aspects of your newsletter service, the more successful it will become as a relationship builder.

178 Provide an enewsletter service

If you're hooked up to the Internet, then you should seriously consider launching an emailed newsletter service that goes out free of charge on a regular basis, say once every two or three months. Not only is this a modern and highly cost-effective method of keeping in touch with your existing customers, but it can also be a great way of initiating a dialogue with prospective customers.

In designing your 'enewsletter', there are two basic formats from which to choose—the informal and the formal. An informal approach simply involves writing an 'extended letter' style of email message that is addressed to each recipient by name. The main ingredients of this style of letter are to adopt a warm, conversational and personal style; to cover a range of different topics such as tips and advice, industry news and information as well as details of your latest special offers; and to always sign off by inviting a response in the form of a request for further information, or for some other kind of customer feedback.

An alternative format is to adopt a more formal layout with a more serious tone. Here's an example (contents page only) of this style of enewsletter:

Roger Brooksbank's Marketing Quarterly

Issue no. 3, July 2001
Editor: Roger Brooksbank, roger@rogerbrooksbank.com
Publisher: The Marketing Improvement Group International

ATTENTION. You are receiving this newsletter in response to your request. If you wish to remove yourself from this mailing list, please follow the instructions at the end of the newsletter. To ensure your privacy, rest assured this mailing list will NOT be made available to any other companies or individuals.

IN THIS ISSUE
1. Welcome
2. An interview with a marketing 'guru'
3. Tips for becoming more creative
4. Book review
5. Wise words for marketers
6. Did you know ... ?
7. Your questions answered
8. Subscriptions management
9. Contact information

In order to generate a list of subscribers for your enewsletter service, start off by encouraging your existing customers to subscribe by explaining the benefits. Next, in order to get prospective customers to subscribe too, you should promote your new enewsletter service by making some reference to it on your business cards, letterheads, brochures and so on. Best of all, if you have a web site, don't forget to include a form so that when visitors are browsing they can subscribe to it on the spot.

179 Use telephone stickers

I picked up this idea from the local branch of a national car rental company. I happened to be in the manager's office one day when I remembered a telephone call I had to make. The manager was kind enough to offer me the use of the telephone and he passed it across to where I was sitting. To my surprise as I started to dial I couldn't help but notice that the handset had two small bright orange stickers on it. Both were in the shape of an arrow. The first one pointed to the earpiece and read:

Spend more time listening here.

and the other sticker pointed to the mouthpiece and read:

Spend less time talking here!

Noticing my amusement and interest in the stickers, the manager proceeded to explain that, because he and his staff spent so much time on the telephone talking to clients, he had come up with this idea as a means of delivering a timely reminder to his staff about the importance of adopting a friendly telephone manner. As if to prove his point, he promptly showed me another telephone in an adjacent office. This time the sticker simply read:

Smile as you dial!

He then went on to give me a handful of stickers that I could use back at the office and give away to my customers, business friends and colleagues. What a bright idea, as well as being an excellent little business gift!

180 Provide video reminders of your hospitality events

Here's a novel way to give your company's hospitality events a lasting impact. By having it professionally videotaped, and giving everyone a copy, you can turn a one-day experience into a treasured and lasting memory. It's the most effective way to make a corporate event truly pay for itself, because it's a permanent reminder of a day when they had lots of fun—but without forgetting who they have to thank for it! Here is what you do.

For this idea to work, your event must be action-based. For example, a day's golf lends itself particularly well to this idea. The video should be based firmly on fun and embarrassment, featuring the best and especially the worst and funniest exploits of each of your guests. Take the opportunity to maximise company name awareness by beginning and ending the video with your logo, and use the voiceover commentary as another subtle reminder. For example, in your commentary, you could refer to the golf tournament as 'The Sandon Group Classic' or whatever sounds good using your own company's name. Above all, keep the video short and sharp, covering only the highlights of the day's events. Last but not least, make it a surprise gift. To continue our example, you could hand out a copy of the video to everyone to round off the day in the 19th hole and send everyone rushing home to watch it!

181 Do more than you get paid for

In our culture we have a strong sense of fair play. It's something that is instilled in us at a very early age and that stays with us for the rest of our lives. Here's a good example of how we can use it to our advantage in our dealings with people:

Some time ago I went to Malta for a business trip, and since I had a day free during the middle of the week, I went for a wander around the shopping mall near my hotel. To my delight, one of the stores was a rather good bookstore so, even though I'd gone out without any money, I went in for a browse, making a beeline for the business section as usual. About two hours later I came out empty handed having sifted through at least 30 or 40 books—and all without even the slightest trace of hostility from the salesgirl, who had been patiently watching over me the whole time. Well, the weather wasn't too good, so I must have spent at least another two hours in there later on that day, sifting through all the rest of the books on the shelf. Once again, the salesgirl didn't bat an eyelid, and she even came over to where I was sitting and asked if I'd like a cup of coffee while I was browsing! Consequently, I'll never forget the overwhelming feeling of guilt I experienced as I walked out of the store empty handed for the second time that day! Now the truth was, I didn't really want any of the books I'd seen. Nevertheless, the sense of obligation I felt to that salesgirl was so strong, I dutifully went back the next day and purchased a book!

So how can we tap into the subtle power of obligation in our dealings with people; and how can we do it ethically? Well, by far the most effective way is to be like the salesgirl in the bookshop and always try to exceed people's expectations of us. The more we put ourselves out for people, the more we'll be appealing to their sense of fair play, and the more they'll become almost obsessed with the desire to do something for us in return. The fact is, when you're serving customers, it always pays to do more than what you get paid for. To put it another way, in business as in life, we get out of a relationship what we put into it—but usually it's returned with interest! Make a note of the following saying—it's one of the key principles of successful relationship marketing:

The more we go out of our way to help our customers get what they want, the more our customers will go out of their way to help us get what we want.

(182) Create a directory of recommended suppliers

Creating a company-branded mini-directory of recommended suppliers is a great way of putting your name across to customers, and keeping it there. Especially when it's distributed to all the other companies' customers featured in the directory as well as your own! Here's how to do it.

Make a list of all the products and services typically used by your customers. Then choose one supplier of each product or service that you consider to be the most reputable. In other words, those companies that you would be prepared to recommend as being the best in the business. (Note that if you're in any doubts about which ones to choose, then your customers will usually be only too pleased to put forward their suggestions.) For example, let's say you sell degreasing equipment to factories, garages, engineering companies and the like; then you'd need to choose one company selling each of the following products and services:

- *hand tools*
- *power tools*
- *protective clothing and safety equipment*
- *nuts, bolts, fixtures and fittings*
- *security equipment*
- *lubricants, engine oils and additives*
- *ball bearings*
- *hydraulic hoses and pipes*

- *overall cleaning services*

- *engine components*

Once you've decided who you'd like to recommend in your directory, telephone them all to make sure they are happy to be included. In addition, take the opportunity to check their contact details and most importantly to find out the number of directories they will require. You see, the key to success with this idea is that you only ever agree to include a supplier in the directory—and to give them x number of copies—on the understanding that in return, they agree to distribute them to their own customers. That way, you are assured of a wide circulation, while at the same time, they get the benefit of being able to pass on a free gift as a thank you to their own customers.

When designing the directory, keep the layout simple and list all the contact details of your recommended suppliers in alphabetical order, category by category. A good tip is to keep your costs down by producing it on a single sheet of laminated cardboard. Above all, don't forget to include your own company in the list and to maximise your name and logo recognition by featuring it prominently elsewhere on the directory. To continue our example, the degreasing company could include their name in the title of the directory as follows:

The 'Best of the Best' Recommended Suppliers Directory
Proudly brought to you by Greaseaters Ltd.

183 Distribute people pictures

If you're in one of those businesses where your service staff are constantly on the telephone with customers, then here's a simple idea that can help personalise their relationships and form even stronger links between your staff and your customers. A 'people picture' is a mini-poster that you hand out to customers. It features head-and-shoulder photographs of all your office-bound customer support staff, together with a few brief details of who they are and their telephone extension numbers. In a business-to-business environment, there's a good chance it will get pride of place in the best advertising site in the world—their office wall! Here's how to do it.

Take passport-style photos of each of your customer support staff and paste them up in the form of a 'rogues gallery', highlighting their names, nicknames, job responsibilities and telephone extension numbers. Prominently feature your main telephone number so that it can easily be read at a glance. Also incorporate your company name and logo, together with a brief sales message. Make sure all your existing customers get one, and if appropriate, maximise its use as a promotional tool by sending it out with your sales literature to new prospective customers or by giving it to your salespeople to hand out.

184 Offer a telephone helpline service

Here's a way of building relationships with your existing customers while at the same time researching the market and widening your potential customer base. Check out the following example:

> 'Le Clinique' is a reputable beauty clinic that has been operating out of the same premises in a busy city shopping centre for many years. It offers a full range of beauty services including facials, manicures, hair removal procedures, skin care programs, massage treatments and suntanning facilities, as well as selling a variety of beauty care products. When the unit next door suddenly became vacant, Felicity, the owner of the business (and herself a well known and highly respected beautician) decided to take the opportunity to expand. She employed two extra beauticians, acquired new equipment and planned to devote a greater proportion of her time to working *on* the business rather than *in* it. As part of her expansion plans, Felicity launched a telephone helpline service. The idea was to capitalise on both her own and her company's reputation by making herself available during daily business hours for anyone to telephone seeking her opinion and advice about their beauty problems. This was achieved by setting up a separate telephone number and promoting it as Le Clinique's new and confidential 'beauty helpline' service. Although to begin with the service was used only infrequently, and mostly by her existing clients, within a few months Felicity found herself fielding more and more calls from women who were not existing clients. In fact, after the first year of operation, an analysis of all the calls received showed that about one-third of them were from non-clients, and that almost half of these had subsequently become new customers of the clinic.

When setting up a helpline service, it's important to promote it as an entirely separate 'stand alone' service and to emphasise that there is no charge, no obligation and no pressure—just an opportunity for people to benefit from your company's knowledge and expertise. Make sure that it is not going to interfere too much with everyday working routines and that one or more staff members, preferably those who are also well known in your business, will be available to handle calls. Needless to say, it will also be necessary to keep a log book so that you are in a position to analyse, on a regular basis, how many calls have been received, from whom, and in relation to what kinds of problem areas.

12

IDEAS FOR CONTROLLING
YOUR COMPANY'S OVERALL
MARKETING EFFORT

Marketing control is the process of measuring how well a company and its staff are performing as time goes by, so that any corrective actions can be taken as and when necessary.

Owner–managers of successful small businesses work on the basis that in a rapidly changing and increasingly competitive world, their strategies and operations should be constantly reviewed. In particular they keep a watchful eye on any newly emerging marketing opportunities or threats.

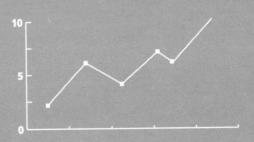

The road to success is
always under construction.

⒙ Use a performance tracker

Things are constantly changing out there—customer needs and wants, new technologies, increasing competition—changing so fast, in fact, that no company's operations can afford to be frozen in time. Not only do you have to be constantly monitoring your marketing performance to see if you're achieving your objectives, but you also need to be constantly checking the business environment to see if your plans are still appropriate in the first place! The easiest way to do all this is to design and use a 'performance tracker'.

A good performance tracker simply consists of a set of standard 'fill in the blanks' forms which you can use on a regular basis to compare events as they unfold in relation to your original plans. In particular, the purpose of a performance tracker is to help you identify any variances between what you had planned for and what is actually happening, so you can make any necessary adjustments to your marketing operations and stay on track.

There are three parts to a well designed performance tracker. The first part, headed *Company Performance*, should relate back to the key marketing objectives you have set for yourself. These should have been broken down into a list of specific targets to be achieved over, say, a monthly planning/control period. This list should include a range of both finance-based performance measures (such as cashflow and profit targets), as well as market-based measures (such as sales volume targets, promotional objectives, customer satisfaction ratings and so on). Adopt a 'fill in the blanks' style of layout so you can write in the actual figure you achieved during the period and compare it, at a glance, with your original target figure. Here's a simplified example of a format to use:

Planning period from_____ to _____	Target	Actual
1 Unit sales (no.) 2 Sales revenue ($) 3 Sales margin (%) etc.		

The second part of your performance tracker, headed *Marketing Intelligence*, should then include plenty of space in which to make a note of any important new information about the marketplace that may have come to light during the period. The type of information to record should relate to issues such as emerging customer needs or competitor activities. Finally, part three should be headed *Action Points*. Whenever you detect any variance between reality and the plan (either positive or negative), and/or you spot some major marketing opportunity or threat on the horizon, it may well be necessary to specify some form of corrective action that needs to be taken.

(186) Conduct win and lose reviews

Imagine a marketing intelligence gathering technique that's quick and easy to do, costs next to nothing and yet provides you with excellent information every time. Well, there is such a technique, and I don't know of any company that couldn't make good use of it. It's the simple idea of following up a sales presentation which has recently been conducted by a member of your sales team (irrespective of the outcome) with a telephone call to find out one of two things. First, why did a customer decide to buy from you (that's called a 'win' review) and second, why did they decide not to buy from you (for obvious reasons, we call that a 'lose' review)? You must admit, finding out the answers to these questions is fundamental to your success! Of course, you don't have to follow up every single sales presentation. Just make sure you do this on a regular basis and in a consistent way, so that as time goes by you can build up a picture of how your proposition to customers can be improved.

(187) Monitor customer satisfaction levels

Here's an example of how a simple piece of customer feedback can lead to dramatic improvements in a company's ability to stay competitive. Some years ago, Malcolm, the owner of a car service garage who'd attended one of my marketing seminars, decided to put some of my recommendations to the test. I'd suggested to him that, although he was exercising tight financial controls, one of the important measures he was ignoring at the time was his ability to keep his customers satisfied so they'd keep coming back to have their cars serviced. However, Malcolm didn't agree. He said he felt he knew his customers so well it would be a pointless exercise. Nevertheless, he promised me he'd do something about it, just to make sure. As you can imagine, I was delighted when, about three months later, he sent me the following letter (paraphrased).

Dear Roger

I finally got around to talking to some of my customers. I met up with about a dozen of them for a chat in the Riverside Hotel and asked, 'How are we doing?'

To my surprise, it seemed that some of them didn't like our opening hours, mostly because we are open at precisely the same time as when they were at work. So, just for a trial period, I've started opening on Saturday mornings, and I'm pleased to report we've been rushed off our feet.

Another thing was that they really didn't like the inconvenience of being left without a car while theirs was in for a service, so I've done a deal with a local car rental company which means that from now on we can offer selected customers a courtesy car.

I was also concerned to hear that when they come to pick up their car after a service, if their final bill was so much as a penny more than our original quote, to them it felt like a rip-off! So I've decided to build a small margin of error into all our quotes from now on. This means our final bills are going to be lower than the original quotes. It should keep everyone happy.

I must admit, I was quite surprised with how well it all went, and so were they. Thanks for the tip.

Yours enthusiastically,

Malcolm

As you can see, one useful method of monitoring customer satisfaction levels is to meet up with a group of your customers to run a focus group. Another would be to conduct a more formal customer satisfaction questionnaire survey, administered either through the post or via the Internet.

Asking your customers 'How are we doing?' on a regular basis serves several purposes. It signals to customers that you're committed to satisfying them and that you value their opinions. In addition, it enables you to pinpoint any problem areas that might need to be addressed, and might even lead to a new product or service idea that hadn't occurred to you before or, better still, create an unexpected opportunity for you to sell more. The point is, you simply must find a way of monitoring customer satisfaction levels, because if you don't keep your customers happy, sooner or later someone else will.

Make the most of sales force reporting procedures

Apart from yourself, if there's anyone else who's really got their finger on the pulse of your marketplace, then it has to be your salespeople. After all, they're out there day in and day out talking to customers and finding out all about their problems and solutions, as well as what the competition is doing. What I'm suggesting is that, if you have salespeople, then potentially they're the ultimate marketing intelligence gathering machine. Wouldn't you agree? So ask yourself, are you making the most of all that knowledge stored away in the minds of your salespeople, and if not, how could you be tapping into it more effectively?

The answer is to improve your sales force reporting procedures. It's a two-step process. The first step is to get all your salespeople together to discuss with them the kind of marketing information, other than that which is purely sales-related, that they should be collecting from now on. For example, this could include finding out how satisfied your customers are with your products and services compared with those of your competitors; feedback regarding the effectiveness of your advertising and promotional campaigns; or any newly emerging customer requirements or new product ideas. The second step involves working with your salespeople to design a report form capable of capturing that information on a regular basis, and most importantly, gaining their commitment to making it happen.

Use standard telephone inquiry pads

Picture the scene. It is late Friday afternoon and the telephone rings. A prospective customer is telephoning for further information about your product or service. Let's say the caller requests that you send them an information pack. Busy with a multitude of other things to clear up by 5.30 p.m., you hurriedly take the caller's details and promise you'll pop the information in the post later on that same afternoon. As soon as you get around to it, however, you immediately realise that you forgot to write down their name (or some other piece of vital contact information). How unprofessional! Yet with the best will in the world, this kind of situation can and does happen all too easily.

One simple solution is to keep a pre-printed telephone inquiry pad next to every telephone in the office. Get the pads printed with a series of questions to ask, so that whoever answers the phone will never again forget to ask all the right questions—not only questions relating to those vital details such as the caller's name and address, but also any other key questions such as: 'How did you hear about us?'

There are a number of benefits to using standard telephone inquiry pads. Quite apart from ensuring that you and your people always come across as highly professional whenever answering the telephone to a prospective customer, this kind of information is crucial to your ability to evaluate the effectiveness of your promotional activities. For example, by analysing the answers given to the question 'How did you hear about us?', you can quickly build up a picture of which promotional methods are working best. As time goes by, you can then compare the effectiveness of one promotional method against another and make more informed decisions about how to maximise the returns from your promotional dollar.

190 Run a marketing intelligence gathering competition

The term 'marketing intelligence gathering' refers to the surveillance of all aspects of a company's competitive environment for the purpose of tracking environmental change and identifying any newly emerging marketing opportunities or threats.

Here's a way to launch a marketing intelligence gathering initiative which will get your staff involved in collecting this kind of information. It's the simple idea of running a short competition among your staff to see who can come up with the best piece of marketing intelligence from the marketplace. To make sure it goes well, make a note of the following suggestions. First, always run this kind of competition over a limited time period, so it really focuses people's efforts. Second, make it absolutely clear that it is purely voluntary and open to everyone in the company, and not just your sales and marketing people. Also, give it a code name, just for fun, such as 'Project Cobra' or something like that, because it helps to capture people's imagination and gets them interested in taking part. Third, design a special entry form for people to fill out for each piece of information they come up with and make it clear that people can post as many entries as they like. At the top of the form, give your people an idea of the kind of information you're looking for, as well as the kind of places they're likely to find it. For example, you could put something like this:

Type of information: (Example—Our major competitor is about to launch a new product)
Source of information: (Example—This information came from one of our existing customers)

In the main body of the form, request that they describe what the new information is and how they discovered it, together with a brief recommendation as to what they think should be done about it. Fourth, make it worthwhile for your staff to take part! Offer a grand prize for the best entry, together with lots of other fun prizes for the runners-up. Lastly, always follow through and act on the information you've been given.

(191) Measure customer loyalty

One of the most important performance measures small companies often overlook is customer loyalty. Perhaps this is understandable because customer loyalty is difficult enough to define, let alone to measure. The dictionary defines loyalty as being 'true, faithful' and having a strong sense of 'commitment, allegiance or duty' towards another person, organisation or government.

In a business context, it is easy to see why the achievement of customer loyalty is often quoted as being even more desirable than the achievement of customer satisfaction. Think about it. A loyal customer would defend you in the face of an attack (even without all the facts), forgive you when things go wrong, tell other people how good you are, and keep on buying from you, come what may! Indeed, you could say that customer loyalty is the only real measure of the strength of the relationships you've built with your customers.

Assuming you sell repeat-purchase products and services and spend a good deal of money, time and effort trying to build relationships with your customers, why not start measuring the extent to which you are successfully breeding customer loyalty? Maybe not for all customers, but at least those who generate the bulk of your profits. After all, you can't buy loyalty, you can only ever really earn it by virtue of your relationship building activities, so it's well worth trying to evaluate and control your abilities in these areas.

In deciding how to go about measuring the concept of customer loyalty, one approach is to measure it according to some aspect of customer behaviour. For example, you can measure one or more of the following:

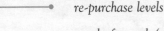

- *re-purchase levels*

- *word-of-mouth (referral) levels*

- *customer longevity rates*

Another approach is to embrace the psychological dimensions of customer loyalty; in other words you can attempt to find out how customers really think and feel about their relationship with your company. To do this, simply telephone each of your key customers on a regular basis. Develop a series of questions which will reveal their true feelings about doing business with you, such as how they feel about your level of:

- *commitment to their business success*

- *trustworthiness as a supplier to their business*

- *integrity in your business dealings*

Customer loyalty is the ultimate measuring stick of how well you are conducting your business relationships, so go ahead and measure it!

 ## Weed out your unprofitable customers

My company once had a customer (I'll call him Mr Bloggs) that I'll not easily forget. Many years ago, Mr Bloggs bought one of our computer systems to help him run his retail newsagency business. At the time, he took advantage of a special offer we were running. For a limited period, we were offering a one-year membership of our 'Customer Care Club' for half price. Membership included a package of benefits including a full set-up and installation service, unlimited training, access to a 24-hour, seven days per week telephone helpline service (newsagents work long hours and at odd times), free software upgrades as they became available, and discounted consumables.

Now whereas the vast majority of customers would require only one or two training sessions before becoming familiar with how to operate the computer, this was not the case with Mr Bloggs. Our training staff must have spent a good two hours a week with him at his shop for at least the first six months after his system was installed! Not only that, but hardly a day would go by without Mr Bloggs monopolising our telephone helpline with one problem or another, and usually complaining. Yes, there's no doubt about it, Mr Bloggs was a very difficult customer indeed, so when his club membership finally came up for renewal, I have to admit that we all rather enjoyed telling him that we couldn't afford to renew it! Then when he complained that it wasn't fair for us to turn him down, we finally decided enough was enough, and insisted that we would pick up the computer and refund his money in full.

The point is, not all customers are necessarily good for business! In fact, most companies have their fair share of Mr Bloggses—those customers who, for one reason for another, are a constant drain on company resources, and who end up costing a fortune to keep. That's why it makes sense to occasionally do a 'profit by customer' analysis.

This means taking a long hard look at your customer base and working out which customers are costing you more money, time and effort to maintain than they're worth. Once identified, you should then seriously consider weeding them out and stopping doing business with them altogether, providing you are legally entitled to do so. The net overall effects in terms of reduced operating costs and improved margins could be substantial. By the way, the best way to get rid of problem customers is to convince them they'd be better off buying from your major competitor!

193 Analyse your moments of truth

The concept of 'moments of truth', as popularised by Jan Carlzon in his book of the same title, provides businesspeople with an excellent method of analysing and controlling the quality of the service that their company is providing to customers. A moment of truth can be defined as any point of interaction (whether face-to-face, by telephone, fax, through the post or by email) that a company has with its customers. The real power of the concept, however, lies in appreciating that a customer's total experience of doing business with a company is made up of a whole series of moments of truth that take place before, during and after a sale. In other words, when joined together, they become the customer's 'chain of experience' of doing business with that company. Just in case you're wondering, these points of interaction are called moments of truth with good reason! Think about it from the customer's point of view—every time they have anything to do with a company, it is a moment of truth about that company's ability to satisfy their service requirements and expectations.

To further illustrate this, put yourself in the shoes of a potential customer for an industrial laser-cutting machine. Let's say you respond to an advertisement in a trade magazine by telephoning to request an information pack. This telephone call now becomes the first moment of truth in your chain of experience in dealing with this company because, depending on how professionally your telephone inquiry is handled, you will begin to form either a positive or a negative impression of them. Assuming the salesperson promises to send you an information pack, the next moment of truth occurs when you receive that information pack. Once again, at this point you will judge them on the basis of the quality of the information pack and covering letter, its contents (relevance to your inquiry), presentation style and so on, not to mention the company's promptness in dealing with your inquiry and despatching your information. Let's say you like what you see and decide to telephone them to arrange a product demonstration. This call then becomes the next moment of truth in the chain. Get the idea?

There are three steps to analysing your company's moments of truth:

STEP ONE—identify them. The best way to do this is to put yourselves in the shoes of a typical new prospective customer. Develop a list of all the points of interaction they would normally have with your company from the moment of first contact all the way through the usual purchasing, selling and service cycle to a point where they are considering a re-purchase of your product or service for a second (or even a third) time.

STEP TWO—assess the quality of your current service provision for each of the moments of truth you have identified. Describe what the customer's expectations are likely to be of what an 'excellent' company should do for them, and then compare these expectations with the reality of what happens.

STEP THREE—design and implement any improvements you could make.

 ## Invest in a computerised marketing database

Database marketing may be defined as the storing of all available information on past, present and prospective customers on a computer for the purpose of supporting all marketing decision-making. As such, it's the ultimate marketing control tool, and I'd advise any company that hasn't already done so to seriously consider investing in one as soon as possible.

A good marketing database system is integrated with a company's accounting system and is flexible enough to enable you to answer the following types of questions, and more:

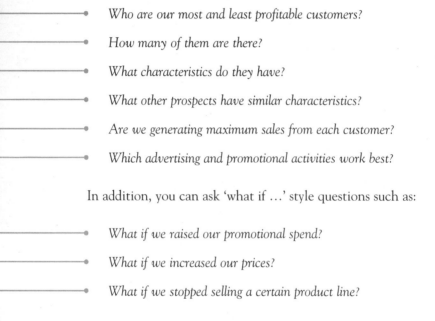

- *Who are our most and least profitable customers?*

- *How many of them are there?*

- *What characteristics do they have?*

- *What other prospects have similar characteristics?*

- *Are we generating maximum sales from each customer?*

- *Which advertising and promotional activities work best?*

In addition, you can ask 'what if ...' style questions such as:

- *What if we raised our promotional spend?*

- *What if we increased our prices?*

- *What if we stopped selling a certain product line?*

As you'll appreciate, there are many benefits associated with using a marketing database system. Making better use of customer information can help you maximise your sales opportunities, reduce your selling costs and improve your customer service and relationship building activities. A powerful combination indeed!

In choosing an appropriate system for your business, be sure to take the advice of a specialist consultant who can help to guide you through the complexities of the buying process. Always start off by mapping out exactly what functions you want it to perform. Next, review all the standard software packages available and conduct a detailed cost–benefit analysis on each one. Finally, before making your selection, always get the vendor to introduce you to some other users, preferably those in businesses similar to your own, so that you can see the system 'in action' for yourself and take the advice of other businesspeople who have already bought one.

Use management observation checklists

One way of ensuring that a consistently high standard of customer service is being delivered by your frontline staff is to use the 'management observation' checklist method. Such an approach is particularly useful in any business where the speed and efficiency of your service provision is a critical aspect of your ability to satisfy customers. By means of example, here's an extract from a checklist used in a fast-food restaurant:

		Yes	No
1	**Greeting the customer**		
1.1	Smile?	☐	☐
1.2	Sincere greeting?	☐	☐
1.3	Eye contact?	☐	☐
2	**Taking the order**	Yes	No
2.1	Order written down?	☐	☐
2.2	Suggestive selling?	☐	☐
2.3	Order checked out loud?	☐	☐
3	**Presenting the order**	Yes	No
3.1	Order properly packaged?	☐	☐
3.2	Order verbalised?	☐	☐
3.3	Order handled with care?	☐	☐
4	**Taking payment**	Yes	No
4.1	Total amount clearly stated?	☐	☐
4.2	Amount received clearly stated?	☐	☐
4.3	Change counted out loud?	☐	☐
4.4	Thanked and asked to come again?	☐	☐

As you can see, the key to an effective checklist is simplicity. The idea is to break down the total service encounter into a series of key steps and from there, to develop a checklist which will enable you to observe and evaluate the standard of service that each of your frontline staff is delivering relative to each step of the process. The checklist should then form the basis of your customer service staff training program, as well as a means by which you can monitor and control the level of your company's service provision.

Encourage frontline staff to monitor their own performance

An effective method of controlling the quality of the service your company delivers to its customers on a day-to-day basis is to encourage frontline staff to monitor and control *themselves*. Providing they have the necessary knowledge about how to perform their job, and they know the standards expected of them, then there's no reason whatsoever why your staff should not take personal responsibility for monitoring the quality of their own service provision. After all, surely the best time to evaluate performance is after every single service encounter, or after every single telephone call received and made, or after every single sales presentation—and who better to do it than the member of staff who has been personally involved in that transaction?

The simplest tool of self-assessment is a checklist. Encourage each member of your frontline staff to develop a simple, personalised checklist that they can use immediately after having dealt with an existing or prospective customer, while the details still remain fresh in their mind. The purpose of the checklist is to enable the staff member to focus upon the key issues and rate their own performance. As long as your staff are able to be totally honest with themselves and are willing to be their own worst critic, then adopting the self-assessment habit can work wonders! Here's an example of a checklist used by a member of staff who is responsible for providing back-up software service and support for clients who have just had a new computer system installed:

    1 Was I responsive, prompt and quick?

    2 Was I competent, knowledgeable and skilful?

    3 Was I courteous, polite and friendly?

    4 Was I understanding, caring and showing empathy?

    5 Was I reliable, dependable and consistent?

Have a 'have your say' day

A 'have your say' day is exactly that: a special day that you put aside, say once or twice a year, when you provide an opportunity for all your customers to tell you exactly what they think about you, your staff and your products and services. If appropriate, you could even extend the invitation to include anyone else who has anything to do with your company, such as your suppliers or your distributors. Quite apart from gaining the kind of information you need in order to run your business more efficiently and effectively, the beauty of this approach is that it's a very public way of signalling to the marketplace your company's commitment to customers. Here's how to go about it.

Obviously, it's imperative that your customers get to know about it before anyone else. This means a few weeks before the day itself, you'll need to send them a personal invitation to have their say. You can do this either by post or, better still, by email (it's much quicker and cheaper). In your letter, start off by thanking them for their valued custom. Next, go on to explain that the purpose behind the 'have your say' day is that you're committed to serving them as best you can, and that on the day, all your staff will be available to receive their feedback on any aspect of your company's operations; be it good, bad or indifferent. As part of the letter, you could even provide customers with a list of issues (such as your product's performance, the standard of your documentation, level of service provision, speed of service response and so on) as a means of prompting their thinking. Sign off by inviting your customers to respond by email, phone, fax or by personal visit on the day, and make a promise that you'll personally ensure that every customer's comments will be followed up and replied to as quickly as possible.

Once your personal invitations have been sent out, it's time to encourage all your staff and salespeople to promote your 'have your say' day by word of mouth. In addition, advertise it in your newsletter, and as a PS on all your company's correspondence leading up to the day itself.

Above all, don't miss the opportunity to try and get some publicity coverage. For example, by writing a brief summary of the day's events, including some statistics on both the level and type of response you received, you might well be sitting on a very successful little news story.

198 Find a way of capturing customer information

How many times have you let customers or visitors walk out of your store or place of business without knowing anything about them: who they are, where they come from, how they found out about your business, or why they even came in the first place? Well, for many owner–managers and especially those operating in a busy retail environment, the truthful answer to this question is that it probably happens all too often, but with good reason. After all, nobody likes to interrogate an unsuspecting customer! Yet, this kind of feedback information is critical to an ability to make good quality marketing decisions. How else are you going to find out which of your promotional activities are working best, or if your target customers are who you think they are, or if their needs and wants are what you thought they were, and so on? The fact is, the more you know about your customers and visitors the better, and no matter how difficult it may be to capture this kind of information, you simply must find a way. Here's an example of how one retailer set about the task, and with astonishing results:

Gardenworld is a garden centre located in an old established residential area at the southern end of a large provincial town. After having successfully grown the business over a period of years, the owners felt that maybe the time was right to open another store at the northern end of town. The assumption was that, while the original store would continue to serve its current customers, a new store would probably attract an entirely different customer base drawn from the fast growing residential suburbs to the north. Before going ahead with a new store, however, it was decided to test out their assumptions, just to be on the safe side. After much discussion, the business owners finally hatched a plan for gathering the information they needed about their current customers and visitor traffic. They would run a one-day 'hidden treasure' competition on a different day of the week over a seven-week period. On the day of each competition, a large street map of the town and its surrounding area would be displayed on the wall adjacent to their checkout/exit area, and all customers and visitors would be invited to stick a pin into the map showing where they lived—blue pins for paying customers, red pins for visitors. Attached to each pin would be a small flag onto which they would write their name and telephone number. Then, at the end of the day, the blue pin closest to the hidden treasure would receive a free 'treasure chest' of garden care products to the value of $250, and similarly, the nearest red pin would receive a $25 gift voucher.

Seven weeks later, the distribution of pins on the seven maps provided an extremely visual picture of Gardenworld's customer catchment area for each day of the week. To the owner's surprise, the pins showed that almost three-quarters of all their customers already came from the new suburbs to the north—a fact which immediately led to a decision to scrap their plans for opening a new store.

There are, of course, many different types of in-store promotions and competitions that can help you capture customer and visitor information. Alongside these, however, other methods to consider include the use of visitors books, or the conducting of some form of in-store market research.

199 Hire a mystery shopper

A 'mystery shopper' is someone who is unknown to you and your staff, and who visits your store or place of business posing as a customer for the specific purpose of evaluating your business relative to a number of pre-defined performance indicators. Of course the beauty of this approach is that the mystery shopper is able to report back to you about exactly how it feels to be a customer of your business. More importantly though, providing the exercise is repeated in a consistent way and on a regular basis, you are also able to gauge how well you and your staff are performing as time goes by, by comparing one report to the next. Here's an example of this idea in action:

> Max runs two 'fast photo' stores (offering one-hour developing and photography equipment) in a large metropolitan area where there are literally dozens of direct competitors. Knowing that a fast, friendly and efficient customer service was critical to the success of his type of business, Max decided that hiring a mystery shopper would be an ideal way of keeping himself and his staff 'on their toes' and on track in these areas. After a little investigation, Max soon found a local company that specialised in providing just the kind of mystery shopper service he was looking for. It was agreed that a trained mystery shopper would visit his stores once per month and that, after each visit, Max would receive a detailed report relating to a range of performance indicators covering store appearance, merchandising and layout, the range and quality of the services offered and the level of selling skills, product knowledge and friendliness of his staff.
>
> Over the next few months, Max was delighted with his mystery shopper program. To his surprise he and his staff found themselves actually looking forward to receiving the reports, which led to the introduction of many new ideas, such as the use of staff name tags, more interesting window displays and a new way of presenting customers with their photos, to name but a few.

As you will appreciate, mystery shopper programs are particularly useful when a company has a number of stores or service points, because the report findings can be used as the basis for ranking each one in order of their performance. Keeping 'league tables' in this way engenders a competitive spirit between staff at different branches, thereby providing yet another spur for them to raise their game in delivering an ever-improving service to customers.

 ## Evaluate every new idea you try

You've probably heard the old maxim: 'I know that about half of all my advertising and promotion is working—the trouble is, I don't know which half!' Well of course, these days, adopting this kind of attitude is no longer an option. You simply must measure and evaluate everything you do and keep modifying and changing those things that aren't working until you find out what does. In today's fast moving and ultra-competitive business environment, the challenge is to continually strive to be better, faster or different—to keep trying out new ideas, and learning from your failures as well as your successes through a process of constant evaluation. Make a note of the following saying:

> *In the end, things always work out best*
> *for those who make the best*
> *of the way things work out.*

This means that every time you try out a new idea, you should discipline yourself to answer the following three questions, regardless of the outcome:

- *What worked well and why?*
- *What could have worked better, and why?*
- *What should I do differently next time?*

This way if you do fail, at least you'll be failing in a forward direction and your inevitable success will be just around the corner.

THE END PIECE

A brief look back at what this book has been about, and what you should do now to maximise its value to you and your business.

The discipline of writing
something down is the
first step towards making
it happen.

I trust this book has been a stimulating read, but please don't put it down just yet! Now is the time for action. If you have not already done so, flick back through the book and make a list of those ideas you think will work best for you in your business. If necessary, think about how you could modify and improve them for maximum effect. Then turn your list into an action plan by putting the ideas into priority order and setting a date for their completion. This will provide you with the starting point for launching a comprehensive marketing improvement program for your business.

In the modern business world, unless you refresh your business with new ideas on a regular basis, you will be left behind by your competitors. So make sure that you return to your action plan periodically, and keep it 'topped up' with a constant stream of your own new ideas. There are many different sources from which to gather new ideas that you should be using on a regular basis. These include:

- *Small business help agencies*
- *Audio programs*
- *Training videos*
- *Books/workbooks*
- *Seminars and conferences*
- *Short courses*
- *The Internet*
- *Trade journals*

In particular, always keep an eye out for any creative new ideas that other businesses (from both inside and outside your industry) are using, and ask yourself how they could be adopted and adapted to work for you in your business.

Well, that's the end of the book, but I hope that it marks just the beginning of a new era of success and prosperity for you and your business. Good luck!

Other publications by the same author

How to Prepare Your Strategic Marketing Plan
A step-by-step audio-workbook guide for owner–managers and marketing directors. Includes 154 pages, 12 worksheets and a corresponding 73-minute audio program.

How to Advertise and Promote Your Business
A step-by-step audio-workbook guide for owner–managers, sales managers and marketing executives. Includes 157 pages, 12 worksheets and a corresponding 63-minute audio program.

How to Become a More Successful Salesperson
A step-by-step audio-workbook guide for owner–managers and professional salespeople. Includes 170 pages, 22 worksheets and a corresponding 63-minute audio program.

Instructor's Resource Packs
These packs are especially designed to accompany the above audio-workbooks, enabling them to be used as the basis for running your own, in-company training programs. Each pack contains a ready-to-use PowerPoint presentation (on disk), and comes with a booklet of instructor's tips.

For further information on these and other products and services visit:
www.rogerbrooksbank.com
or:
email roger@rogerbrooksbank.com
Tel (+64) (7) 854 9691
Fax (+64) (7) 854 9652